I0161371

יום הבכורים

YOM HaBIKKURIM
THE DAY OF FIRSTFRUITS
RESURRECTION DAY

Rabbi Jim Appel

יום הבכורים Yom HaBikkurim
The Day of FIRSTFRUITS
RESURRECTION DAY
Appointed Times Series - FIRSTFRUITS
Copyright © 2020 by Rabbi James Appel

Printed in the USA ISBN 978-1-941173-442

1. Jewish Holidays 2. Messianic Judaism 3. Resurrection Day

Published by

Olive **P**ress Messianic and Christian Publisher
www.olivepresspublisher.com
olivepressbooks@gmail.com

Messianic & Christian Publisher

Our prayer at Olive Press is that we may help make the Word of Adonai fully known, that it spread rapidly and be glorified everywhere. We hope our books help open people's eyes so they will turn from darkness to Light and from the power of the adversary to God and to trust in ישוע Yeshua (Jesus). (From II Thess. 3:1; Col. 1:25; Acts 26:18,15 NRSV and CJB).

Other books by Rabbi Jim Appel:

Messianic Judaism Class Teacher Book, Student Book,
and five *Answer Books.*

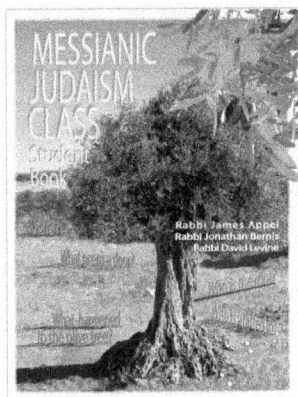

Rosh Hashanah, Yom Teruah, The Day of Sounding the Shofar

Yom Kippur, The Day of Atonement

Pesakh, Passover

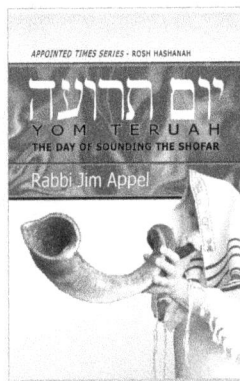

CONTENTS

CONTENTS IN DETAIL

GLOSSARY

יום **Yom** *yohm* day

בכורים **Bikkurim** *bee-kur-eem'* Firstfruits

חג **Khag** (also spelled Chag) *khahg* (The a is an ah sound. Again the kh is a guttural sound. There is no ch sound in Hebrew.) holiday, festival, feast

ישוע **Yeshua** *Yeh-shoo'-ah* - Jesus' original Hebrew Name, which basically means Salvation and is pronounced almost exactly the same as the Hebrew word for salvation ישועה.

מועד **Moad** *moh'-odd* - Appointed Time, Biblical Holiday

מועדים **Moadim** *moh-ah-deem'*- plural of Moad

ברית חדשה **Brit Khadashah** (also spelled B'rit Hadasha or Chadasha) *B'reet Khah-d'-shah'* (Again the kh is a gutteral sound.) - **New Covenant** (sometimes referring just to the Covenant itself, sometimes to the whole New Testament.)

CE - common era (same as AD)

BCE - before the common era (same as BC)

INTRODUCTION

YESHUA'S RESURRECTION OCCURRED ON A JEWISH BIBLICAL HOLIDAY

Yes, It's True!

Yes, you read the title right. Resurrection Day is a Jewish Biblical Appointed Time. How do I know? Well, I am Jewish. I was raised Jewish. I grew up celebrating all the Jewish holidays with my maternal grandparents who were Jewish Orthodox. After God revealed to me in my 30s that Yeshua is our Messiah, I have not stopped learning about all the connections of things in the Torah to Yeshua,[1] especially all the *Moadim*.[2]

Let me tell you a little more about myself and our congregation. I have been the leader of Congregation Shema Yisrael in Rochester, New York since 1996. (*Shema Yisrael* is Hebrew and means *Hear O Israel*.) We are a group of believers in Yeshua. About half of us are Jewish. We call ourselves a Messianic Jewish congregation. We use the term *Messianic* because we believe that Yeshua/Jesus is the Messiah of Israel and of the whole world, and that only

---

1   *Yeshua* is Jesus' Hebrew Name and means *Salvation*
2   Hebrew for *Appointed Time*

through receiving the atoning sacrifice of Yeshua can we be forgiven of our sins and enter into a personal relationship with God.

Our main purpose as a congregation is to reach the Jewish people with the Good News of Messiah Yeshua. But along with that, part of our calling is also to educate the rest of the Body of Messiah on the Jewish roots of Christianity to enrich their understanding of the Bible.

Replacement Theology is Wrong

Why isn't the understanding of the Jewish roots present in most of Christianity today? Well, in 325 CE, the church, under the influence of the Roman Emperor Constantine, outlawed all Jewish practices.

In Acts 15, the Jewish leaders of the new congregations who believed in Yeshua as the Messiah (thus we call them Messianic) were wrestling with the question of what to do with Gentiles who were coming to this new faith. From the leading of the Holy Spirit, they chose not to restrict the Gentiles, not to put extra burdens on them, but to receive them with open arms into the fold.

> Acts 15:28-29 *For it seemed good to the Ruach HaKodesh* (Holy Spirit) *and to us not to lay any heavier burden on you than the following require-ments: 29 to abstain from what has been sacri-ficed to idols, from blood, from things strangled, and from fornication. If you keep yourselves from these, you will be doing the right thing.*

Three hundred years later when the majority of the believing leaders were Gentile, and the question of what to do with Jewish believers came up, their response was quite different. They ruled that Jewish believers must give up all things Jewish and punished them if they didn't. Replacement Theology became the prevalent belief, which wrongly says that God has rejected the Jewish people and the church replaces Israel. It is quite sad to us. Actually, it was tragic. It caused centuries of mistreatment and outright persecution of Jewish people by the church, even to the extent of being one of the things that influenced the Holocaust in Europe in the 1930's and 1940's.

If the Gentile church leaders in the 300's CE would have honored and treated the Jewish believers as well as the Jewish leaders treated and honored the Gentile believers in Acts, history could have been much better.

Here is a large excerpt from our *Messianic Judaism Class* book about the history after Acts 15 leading up to that fateful 300 CE ruling, and then beyond to current times. This excerpt starts with question #126 on page 150 in the Teacher Book, page 117 in the Student Book.[3]

> In Rabbi Shaul's (Apostle Paul's) day there were congregations of Messianic Jews in Israel and congregations of Jews and Gentiles in the Diaspora with Messianic Jewish Leadership in Jerusalem until Rome destroyed Israel in 70 CE.
>
> [The] surviving Jewish people were dispersed throughout the Roman Empire and persecuted.
>
> The Jewish leadership of Messiah's body was dispersed.
>
> There was great persecution of Jewish and Gentile believers by the Romans.
>
> The Gospel spread throughout the Roman Empire.
>
> People thought Judaism would disappear.
>
> Replacement Theology took over: The Church was the New Israel
> It was a very nice, self satisfying theology that made [theologians of that time] feel good and important. [Their identity became "God's Chosen People"] They became very attached to [that identity].

3 *Messianic Judaism Class Teacher Book* and *Student Book*, Rabbi Jim Appel, Rabbi Jonathan Bernis, and Rabbi David Levine, Olive Press Publisher, 2011.

Gentile leadership increased because the number of Gentiles in the Body increased.

But, non-Messianic Judaism did not disappear. It flourished in the Roman Empire, contradicting Replacement Theology, and competing with Messianic Jews for the hearts of the Jewish people.

The existence of non-Messianic Jews was an affront to the theologians. They couldn't live with it. It refuted their self image of being God's chosen people.

So, they began to hate Judaism which led to hatred of non-Messianic Jews by church leaders and to [the] cutting off the church from its Jewish roots.

Also, because of persecution of Jews by Rome, Gentile believers did not want to be identified as Jews.

Around 300 CE, the Roman Emperor, Constantine, became a believer.

He took over the Body of Messiah at the Council of Nicea.

He ended persecution of the believers [which was wonderful].

[But] he turned the Body from a Jewish movement to a Roman military structure, and [he and] the church leadership outlawed Jewish practices within the Body.

What happened to the olive tree in Romans 11?[4]

[In Rabbi Sha'ul's analogy,] one particular grafted-in branch broke itself off from the root and planted itself in the ground.

It tried to sprout roots which would reach the water table.

It also broke all the other branches off the root. ....

What happened to the world?[5]

For hundreds of years, the Dark Ages prevailed.

The Reformation was a break in this branch's power.

Branches of the church broke away from the Catholic tree.... [and] planted themselves in the ground. ... [But] they're designed to be branches, not roots.

The sap only comes from the ... deep, strong root which the wild branches are meant to be grafted into.

---

4 Question #127 on p. 151 in the Teacher Book, p. 117 in the Student Book.
5 Question #129 on p. 152 in the Teacher Book, p. 118 in the Student Book.

This is an ongoing offense by the Gentile Church against Messianic Jews, [Forbidding] Jewish practices, such as: Shabbat, Feasts of the Lord, ... and Kashrut (Kosher eating).

[But we are seeing a change!! Praise the Lord!]

The Gentile church is turning toward repentance of anti-Semitic treatment of Jews. But [some] are [still] not aware that the root of anti-Semitism is the breaking off the branches from the Jewish root.

If the Church had maintained its Jewish roots, how could it have become anti-Semitic? ....

How is God re-grafting in the broken off branches?[6]

.... He's causing Messianic Judaism to flourish.

He is awakening in Gentile believers a hunger for an understanding of their Jewish roots.

He's bringing new revelation in the Gentile Church that God is still interested in Appointed Times for the entire Body. .....

We Messianic Jews are receiving a deeper understanding of His Appointed Times.

He's bringing a spirit of repentance to the Gentile church: for its treatment of Jews [and] for cutting itself off from its Jewish roots.

*****

The truth from Scripture is that if you are a non-Jewish believer, you have been grafted in to the Olive Tree which is Israel, not the other way around (Romans 11).

Romans 11:18 ...don't boast as if you were better than the branches! However, if you do boast, remember that you are not supporting the root, the root is supporting you.

God has not rejected the Jewish people or Israel.

Romans 11:1-2 (TLV) I say then, God has not rejected His people, has He? May it never be! For I too am an Israelite, of the seed of Abraham, of the tribe of Benjamin.2 God has not rejected His people whom He knew beforehand.

---

6 Question #131 on p. 152 in the Teacher Book, p. 118 in the Student Book..

Romans 11:22-24 *So take a good look at God's kindness and his severity: on the one hand, severity toward those who fell off; but, on the other hand, God's kindness toward you — provided you maintain yourself in that kindness! Otherwise, you too will be cut off! 23 Moreover, the others, if they do not persist in their lack of trust, will be grafted in; because God is able to graft them back in. 24 For if you were cut out of what is by nature a wild olive tree and grafted, contrary to nature, into a cultivated olive tree, how much more will these natural branches be grafted back into their own olive tree!*

The re-birth of the nation of Israel in 1948 and God's protection of Israel against all odds from many attacks from surrounding nations since then, plus the growing number of Messianic Jewish congregations around the world since the 1960's and those becoming an influence in some governments and in Israel society are living proof of the truth of Romans 11.

The Purpose for My Books

My purpose for writing my *Appointed Time* series of books, besides to help Jewish believers see that all the Moadim/Appointed Times point to our Messiah Yeshua, is to also help non-Jewish believers gain an understanding of the Jewish roots upon which our common faith is built.

Ephesians 3:6 *that in union with the Messiah and through the Good News the Gentiles were to be joint heirs, a joint body and joint sharers with the Jews in what God has promised.*

As a joint heir, you have an inheritance. It is the spiritual, historical heritage of Israel. One of our goals as a congregation is to restore you to your inheritance, while our other main goal is to bring Jewish people to the revelation that Yeshua is the Messiah and to accept and receive Him. In this book, I want to reveal the Biblical Jewish connection to Resurrection Day.

Yeshua's Resurrection was God's confirmation that Yeshua's crucifixion was for a purpose, that it was part of God's plan to bring in the New Covenant and His Kingdom. As part of His plan, He designed that the Resurrection occurred on the exact, significant day He purposed for it.

So Resurrection Day is the last of a series of three Biblical holidays which are very important on God's calendar. If you were raised in the church, you might be thinking Maundy Thursday, Good Friday, and Easter Sunday. But, none of these days are mentioned in the Bible by name. The King James Version, in Acts 12:4, uses the word *Easter*, but it is actually translating the Greek word *Pascha*, which is the Greek transliteration of the Hebrew word *Pesakh* which means *Passover*. The New King James Version and the New International Version use *Passover* in that verse. The name Easter was not used until more than 1000 years after the New Testament was written. Why and how it became a Christian term for Passover and Resurrection Day is a long story, and there are lots of theories and opinions that we don't want to get into here. We want to focus on what is in God's written Word.

So what are the three Biblical holidays? In Leviticus 23:5-9, the first two days mentioned are Passover and the Feast of Unleavened Bread. Then verses 10-11 tell us that the day after the Sabbath, or the Sunday during the Passover week is Firstfruits.

So, on the Jewish calendar, we celebrate Yeshua's Resurrection Day on the Biblical Appointed Time of Firstfruits. Let's find out more about that holy day, that Moad.

16

Chapter 1

BARLEY HARVEST AND FIRSTFRUITS OFFERING

Yeshua Fulfilled Torah And Tradition

If we look at Leviticus 23 where all the *Moadim* are listed, we see that **Pesakh, Passover** is the first in a series of **three spring *Moadim***, three Appointed Times that are Biblically and prophetically significant. In my book titled, *Pesakh, Passover*, we looked at how Yeshua fulfilled the commandments and the traditions concerning Passover.

The Passover Lamb was to be slaughtered on the 14th day of the month and its blood placed on the doorposts so that the tenth plague would "pass over" the Israelites' households.

Yeshua died on the Cross on the 14th day of the month at the exact same time that the Passover lambs were being sacrificed.

Yeshua's life was sacrificed and His blood was placed on the Cross to cause the plague of eternal death to "pass over" those who receive Him as their Passover lamb.

At our Pesakh Seder, Passover meal, we also show how Yeshua even fulfilled the traditions which developed in obedience to the commandment to eat unleavened bread. We show that the Matzah looks striped, bruised, pierced, and is broken just like Yeshua was striped, bruised, pierced, and His skin was broken. Then we show that the Afikomen is wrapped and hidden away, just like Yeshua's body was wrapped, then hidden away in the tomb.

We also explain that Yeshua used the third cup out of the four traditional cups of a Seder, the Cup of Redemption along with Matzah to establish the New Covenant communion ceremony.

The second spring *Moad* (Appointed Time) is the seven-day **Feast of Unleavened Bread**. Yeshua fulfilled the commandment concerning Unleavened Bread, too. Leaven represents sin and He was without sin.

Third Spring Moad, Appointed Time, HaBikkurim, Firstfruits

The third spring Moad happens on "the day after the Sabbath."

> Leviticus 23:10-11 *Speak to Bnei-Yisrael (Sons of Israel) and tell them: When you have come into the land which I give to you, and reap its harvest, then you are to bring the omer of the firstfruits of your harvest to the kohen. 11 He is to wave the omer before ADONAI (the LORD), to be accepted for you. On the morrow after the Shabbat, the kohen (priests) is to wave it.*

The bringing of the firstfruits to the cohen (priests, also spelled kohen) happened as a procession. (Remember that for later.) The *sheaf* or *Omer* of firstfruits was from the first of the barley harvest. The first crop that comes up in Israel is barley. Let's look at the Hebrew words for *sheaf* and *Firstfruits*.

Sheaf - עֹמֶר *o-mehr, a heap, a sheaf; also an omer, as a dry measure.*

Firstfruits - רֵאשִׁית *rey-sheet - the first,* in place, time, order or rank (specifically a *firstfruit):—beginning, chief* (-est), *principal thing.* Called *ray-sheet* here. It is similar to *B'ree-sheet* – in the Beginning. It is how the Bible begins in Genesis 1:1. It can apply to the first of anything.

So where did we get the name *HaBikkurim* for Firstfruits? It is first mentioned in Exodus 23.

> Exodus 23:16a *Also you are to observe the Feast of Harvest, the firstfruits of your labors that you sow in the field,*

There it uses the word, בְּכוּרֵי *bikkuri* ("i" is pronounced "ee," *beekkuree*), *firstfruit,* the *firstfruits* of the crop. It applies specifically to the crops of the Land. The climate in Israel is a warm climate. They have their barley harvest in early spring.

Barley Harvest

Barley grows in our area, and maybe in yours. According to *Wikipedia*, "barley serves as a major animal feed crop. In ranking cereal crops in the world, barley is usually around the fourth in quantity produced and in the area of cultivation (usually around 560,000 km²)." So there's lots of barley out there. It is still used as a food staple for people in the Middle East. The interesting thing about barley is that it is very similar to what we call winter wheat where I live. Barley is planted in the autumn when the ground has been moistened by the "early rains," and it stays in the ground all winter. Then it is the first crop to come up in the spring and ripens earlier than wheat.

The historian, Josephus, gave us some important information about the barley harvest. He wrote about it in his history of the Jewish people during the time of the Temple. He said that "they take a handful of the ears, and dry them, then beat them small, and purge the barley from the bran; they then bring one tenth deal [that's the omer] to the altar, to God: and, casting one handful of it upon the fire, they leave the rest for the use of the priest."

The reason that tidbit is significant is because of that phrase in there: to "purge the barley from the bran." A barley farmer will tell you it has to be ripe or you can't get the bran apart from the grain. It must have ripened to be able to do that. So the challenge was for people in those days, and would be today if we still did it this way, how could you be sure it was going to be ripe on this Appointed Time, on this day each year, so that you could make this offering? Because if it wasn't ripe, you couldn't do it, and this was a command of God.

Biblical Lunar Calendar Difficulties

The difficulty was there especially because the Biblical calendar is lunar. It does not synchronize with the seasons. It shifts around relative to the seasons. The seasons are regulated by the sun going around the earth, not by the moon. The moon doesn't go around the earth in exactly an integral number of times in a year. It goes around 12.5 times instead of 12 times. Therefore, if you have a lunar calendar, your months shift.

Today, the Jewish authorities have remedied this by designing a calendar with a 19-year cycle. This calendar prevents the shift of seasons by making seven out of the 19 years into leap years. That's what keeps the Appointed Times from shifting away from the correct seasons.

If you've noticed, the Muslim celebration of Ramadan moves to different times of the year because their calendar is lunar and doesn't have leap years, so it shifts around. Ramadan is in the fall, then slowly moves backwards year by year to summer, then it gradually keeps shifting backwards to spring, etc., all the way backwards around the seasons until it is in the fall again.

But in the modern Jewish calendar, in every 19 year cycle, there are seven leap years, and in a leap year, a whole month is inserted in the spring. A second Adar month, the last month in the Biblical year (the month before the Passover month of Nissan) is inserted. If they didn't add those leap months, then the Appointed Times would shift back every year until the Spring Moadim would be in the winter, then fall, then in the summer, then back to spring. Around and around backwards they would move. That's why you notice that the Moadim every once in a while will suddenly leap forward a whole month. Now you know why.

The Lunar Calendar In Biblical Times

However, in Biblical times, they didn't have leap years in their lunar calendar. I recently learned an amazing thing that kind of turns things upside down in terms of how we think of agriculture and the calendar. I think this is really a fascinating thing concerning the barley. God commanded to begin the months on each new moon. They were to watch for the first sliver of the moon to know when the month begins. Lunar eclipses happen when there's a full moon. That happens in the middle of a month. People talk about the Passover moon. Passover is on the 14th of the month so the moon is always full. Most of the Moadim are on or near full moon. Yom Teruah, Rosh Hashanah, Feast of Trumpets is an exception. It is on the new moon.

So, the new moon is the beginning of the month. But you would have to figure out which month is the first month of the year for the barley to be ripe. What I understand happened back in those days was that they observed the barley for the earliest new "tender ears." If you look at barley that is not ripe, you can see on the grains little green protrusions that stick up. They're called ears on the barley grain, like Mickey Mouse ears. Barley farmers know that these tender ears of the barley appear around two weeks before the barley is ripe. So what they used to do is they would observe the barley growing. When the "tender ears" appeared, they would wait for the next new moon, and they would start their new year on that next new moon.

So that would be an unknown number of days, and New Year would be an unknown time until that moment. But whatever number of days it was, two weeks later, the barley would be ripe. So it would definitely be ripe by the middle of that month, and there would be time for it to be dried, beaten (according to what Josephus wrote), and ready for the Firstfruits offering, which would be offered a few days after the full moon of that month.

The Barley Harvest Determined the Beginning

So the following new moon became the beginning of the new year, and they didn't insert leap months. They just waited for the first tender barley ears to appear. The name of the first month, Aviv, actually means "tender ears" and has also come to mean "spring." Then they would count fifteen days from that next new moon to celebrate Passover. And on the day after the Shabbat after Passover, they would offer the Firstfruits offering. By then the barley kernels would be ripe enough to be dried, beaten, and offered as Firstfruits the correct way (per Josephus' description).

I think this is so amazing because the barley crop was determining when the new year started. Today it is the calendar that determines when we plant things. But back then the crops actually determined the calendar. The ripening barley actually determined which new moon began the year.

Did I lose you there? Let me explain it further because It is so different from how we live today. If you have a garden, the calendar tells you when it is okay to plant, right? In the area where I live, everyone knows not to plant anything before Memorial Day because you might get a frost. So we go by the calendar to know when to plant. But in Biblical times, it was just the opposite, the plants told them when to start the calendar. The barley harvest determined New Years Day! (They couldn't plan very far ahead for New Year's celebrations, could they?) I think it is amazing that God provided that so people would have a way to keep the calendar synchronized with the seasons rather than doing all this with adding in of the leap months.

Omer Firstfruit Offering, A Joyous Festival

Leviticus 23:11 *He is to wave the omer before ADONAI, to be accepted for you....*

This is the cohen, the priest taking the firstfruits and waving it and burning some of it on the altar. So that first sheaf or omer was given to Adonai. Here is another agricultural thing that is important to understand. If you haven't done any farming, you might not know this. When a farmer raises a crop, especially a grain crop, the first grains that become ripe, are the strongest stock because they ripened first. So he gathers those and saves them for seed for the next year because that is going to be the best grain. Those are the seeds you want to plant the next year because those are the seeds from the strongest plants.

So, this was an act of faith. The farmers were told to take that first grain that was supposed to be the best and give a large portion of it to the Lord on Firstfruits. So you can see that it took faith and obedience. "I'm taking some of my best that I would normally save to plant, that would give me the next year's best crop, and I'm going to give it to You, Lord." "We're giving You the best seeds, Lord, and we're trusting You to bless the rest of the harvest." It was an act of faith that the Lord would bless the rest of the crop. It was offered in faith that a bountiful harvest would follow.

> Leviticus 23:11 ... *On the morrow after the Shabbat, the kohen is to wave it.*

Leviticus 23 verses 5-8 are where the commandments for Passover are. So this verse is referring back to Passover. So, Biblically, Firstfruits is always on the day after the Sabbath during the week of Passover or Feast of Unleavened Bread. (More on that in a later chapter.)

> Leviticus 23:14 *You shall eat neither bread nor parched grain nor fresh grain until the same day that you have brought an offering to your God....*

This is where it becomes a joyous festival because what was happening was people were eating stored grain from the previous year up to that date. By that time that grain was getting old. It would have begun to lose its flavor. It might have even started to become moldy. But no matter how old it tasted, they had to wait until after the day of Firstfruits to begin eating the delicious, fresh, new grain. So this was a time of great celebration, rejoicing that God has blessed us. The new grain is coming in, and we can make barley bread out of this new grain and eat it. Following the Firstfruits offering, the markets would have been flooded with the new crop, and everybody would be buying new grain and making things from it. So you can see why they would be celebrating. They would be rejoicing that they had fresh grain.

You know, if the weather conditions didn't work, if they didn't get rain at the proper times, there wouldn't be enough new grain, so this was a celebration. This was a pretty significant day in Temple times. It was all about what you ate and when the year would start, and was a time of rejoicing in all those things.

There were other offerings commanded for Yom HaBikkurim.

> Exodus 23:12-13 *On the day when you wave the omer you are to offer a male lamb without blemish, one year old, as a burnt offering to ADONAI. 13 The grain offering with it should be two tenths of an ephah of fine flour mixed with oil—an offering made by fire to ADONAI for a soothing aroma. Its drink offering with it should be a quarter of a gallon of wine.*

They were to bring a lamb as a burnt offering. This is for atonement for unintentional sins, and for an expression of devotion, surrender, and commitment to the Lord. They were also supposed to bring the usual flour mixed with oil as a grain offering. This is for recognition of God's goodness and provision. Accompanying the grain offering, as always, there was to be wine as a drink offering, which is a symbol of joy. The firstfruits is to be offered with joy and gladness. It was celebrated with a procession of joy and praise as the offerings were brought to the cohenim, the priests.

In Temple times, people stayed on after Pesakh to celebrate this holiday of Yom HaBikkurim in Jerusalem. On Firstfruits morning, there would be a huge procession of people, each family with a lamb and flour and oil and wine, and also carrying their basket filled with their first fruit omer (sheaf) of grain. They would be carrying these things into the Temple where they would present it all to the cohanim (priests). So there were always many crowds of people still in Jerusalem on Yom HaBikkurim.

Now let's move to the New Covenant. What significant event occurred on Yom HaBikkurim in the New Covenant? Yes, Yeshua's Resurrection. Early that morning while it was still dark, there was an earthquake and the stone was rolled away, revealing the empty tomb! This occurred on a Moad, a Biblical Appointed Time, commanded by Elohim Himself! It is not coincidence. It is by God's design that His Son would rise from the dead on Firstfruits morning.

Blank Stares

Now what's really interesting to me about this holiday is if you were to go out into the Jewish community and ask people about Firstfruits, you would get blank looks. I've done it. You get blank stares. Most American Jewish people don't even know that this holiday exists, except that it marks the beginning of the Counting of the Omer, counting the 50 days leading to Shavuot, Pentecost, as commanded in Leviticus.

> Leviticus 23:15-16 *And you shall count for yourselves from the day after the Sabbath, from the day that you brought the sheaf of the wave offering: seven Sabbaths shall be completed. 16 Count fifty days...*

Now we Jewish people have taken this verse literally and have always actually counted the days, much like we took putting His Word on our doorposts and gates literally. So that commandment is obeyed by religious Jewish people. But the Moad of HaBikkurim (Firstfruits), totally is not kept in modern Judaism, even though it is commanded in the Torah and is supposed to be a great day of celebration. I believe part of the reason is to distance the Jewish community from the New Covenant. Ever since the time of the book of Acts, the non-believing, traditional Jewish authorities, have wanted to keep their people from seeing any connection between what Yeshua came to do and Judaism.

Timing Disagreement with Traditional Judaism

So in our congregation, we Messianic Jewish believers do observe Yom HaBikkurim. We do give a Firstfruits offering in faith, believing God will bless our finances the rest of the year. We also rejoice, but for much more than just the blessing of our finances. We celebrate and rejoice first and foremost in the Resurrection of our Savior and Messiah Yeshua. In addition to calling it Yom HaBikkurim, we call it Resurrection Day!

Then we begin the Counting of the Omer on that day as commanded in the Torah, which should be in line with the non-Messianic Jewish counting. However, if you look on a traditional Jewish calendar, the count starts on the second day of Unleavened Bread (Matzah), on whatever day of the week that falls. On the years that the second day of Matzah lands on a Sunday, our count starts the same day as traditional Jewish calendars. Thus on those years, we celebrate Shavuot at the same time as the rest of the Jewish community.

The difference is based on differing interpretations of this phrase in Leviticus.

> Leviticus 23:15 (CJB) *"'From the day after the day of rest...*

The day of rest can be the Saturday Shabbat during the week of Matzah, but it could also be the first day of Matzah (which is also the day of Passover) because God commanded that it must be a Shabbat. The non-Messianic Jewish community has decided that this phrase is referring to the first day of Matzah. We Messianic Jews have chosen the Saturday Shabbat during the week of Matzah.

So one year, I decided to read the traditional Jewish readings that have been laid out, a specific reading for every day of Unleavened Bread. So I got out my interlinear Bible, and I looked for what to read that particular day. It was Leviticus 22:26-23:44. Because it started in chapter 22 and I was reading it in Hebrew, it didn't occur to me that I had reached the next chapter (because in the Hebrew, there are no chapter or verse markings). I know Leviticus 23 so well in Hebrew that I probably would not have re-read it. I probably would've said, "Oh, I'm not going to bother to read that, I know it already." So I started reading it in Hebrew, thinking it was some other section in chapter 22 about the Moadim that I hadn't read for awhile. So I wasn't reading like "Oh yea, I know this, and oh I know that." Instead I was really focusing on it as I read it.

I was using my interlinear Bible that has the English right below the Hebrew. So what I do is I cover up the English and try to understand the Hebrew. If I don't understand a certain word, I look down and see what the English word is. But the Hebrew in that passage has very familiar words, so it was really easy for me to read it all in Hebrew without looking at the English. And I was stunned!!! I was just amazed! I wasn't thinking about the calendar or anything at that moment. But when I read it in the Hebrew, it was so clear! It was completely clear that Firstfruits and the start of the Count of the Omer should be on a Sunday, the way we Messianics do it!

So here on the next page is Leviticus 23:15-16 in Hebrew.

וּסְפַרְתֶּם לָכֶם, מִמָּחֳרַת הַשַּׁבָּת, מִיּוֹם הֲבִיאֲכֶם, אֶת-עֹמֶר
הַתְּנוּפָה: שֶׁבַע שַׁבָּתוֹת, תְּמִימֹת תִּהְיֶינָה.
עַד מִמָּחֳרַת הַשַּׁבָּת הַשְּׁבִיעִת, תִּסְפְּרוּ חֲמִשִּׁים יוֹם; וְהִקְרַבְתֶּם
מִנְחָה חֲדָשָׁה, לַיהוָה.

It says in Hebrew, *"you are to count mi-makharet ha-Shabbat (from the day after the Shabbat),"* then it goes on, *"the day that you bring the sheaf to wave."* Then it says, *"sheva shabbatot (seven Shabbats) shall be completed for you."* So this verse 15 alone is very clear that you are supposed to start the count on the day after Shabbat. Verse 16 is where it really gets interesting. *"ohd mih-mah-khar-raht (until the day after) ha-shabbat hashvi'im (the seventh Shabbat)."* This is what really got me because what it is saying is *"until the day after seventh Shabbat"*!! There's no ambiguity to that. It's got to be on the day after a Shabbat, not seven weeks later on a Wednesday. It finishes by saying, *tispru khamishim yom (count fifty days) and bring a new grain offering to Adonai."*

That is what got me there in verse 16. *"ohd mih-mah-khar-raht (until the day after) ha-shabbat hashvi'im (the seventh Shabbat)."* There's no other way you should translate that. I hope you can see as I did how clear it is in the Hebrew. And also that the fiftieth day must also be a "day after the Shabbat." The day that you start the count is the day that you do the wave offering which is on the day after Shabbat and then 50 days later, Shavuot is supposed to be on the day after the seventh Shabbat.

The Tree of Life Version (TLV), that we use for the Tanakh Scriptures in this book, is as close to the Hebrew as you can get while keeping correct English grammar and syntax, as you can see here.

Leviticus 23:15-16 (TLV) *Then you are to count from the morrow after the Shabbat, from the day that you brought the omer of the wave offering, seven complete Shabbatot. 16 Until the morrow after the seventh Shabbat you are to count fifty days, and then present a new grain offering to ADONAI.*

The New Kings James Version (NKJV) also is very accurate.

Leviticus 23:15-16 (NKJV) *And you shall count for yourselves from the day after the Sabbath, from the day that you brought the sheaf of the wave offering: seven Sabbaths shall be completed. 16 Count fifty days to the day after the seventh Sabbath; then you shall offer a new grain offering to the LORD.*

Keeping the Two Separate

Then I took a look at two Jewish translations to try to figure out why they make it a different day. The first one is the Complete Jewish Bible. You need to understand that the Tanakh section of it is not a translation from the original by David Stern. He just took an existing out-of-copyright Jewish translation and updated the pronunciations of the names and some out-dated English words in it. (It is only the New Covenant that he translated from the original.) So both of the following are the standard Jewish Publication Society (JPS) translation from 1917. They are a little different because of David Stern's updating from the JPS English, etc.

Leviticus 23:16 (CJB) *until the day after the seventh week; you are to count fifty days; and then you are to present a new grain offering to ADONAI.*

Leviticus 23:16 (JPS 1917) *even unto the morrow after the seventh week shall ye number fifty days;*

and ye shall present a new meal-offering unto the
LORD.

Notice the switch from "the day after the Shabbat" to "the day after the seventh week." It doesn't say "week" "shavuah" there at all. It says "Shabbat." And yet they've changed it to week. So you can see there's something up here. (In Hebrew, there's a big enough difference between "Shabbat" שַׁבָּת and "shavuah" שָׁבוּעַ. Only two of the Hebrew letters are the same.) There sure seems to be an intentional switching—an intentional making of the translation such that it supports the Jewish community's position that it should be the day after Passover that you begin the Omer count.

As noted above, the NKJV and the TLV translate it very accurately from the Hebrew.

> Leviticus 23:16 (NKJV) *Count fifty days to the day after the seventh Sabbath; then you shall offer a new grain offering to the LORD.*

> Leviticus 23:16 (TLV) *Until the morrow after the seventh Shabbat you are to count fifty days, and then present a new grain offering to ADONAI.*

The Torah clearly makes the days of Firstfruits and Shavuot both Sundays. To me the Hebrew couldn't be anymore clear than that. So, if we follow the Hebrew, which we in the Messianic Movement do, it would be very clear that the day that the count starts would be on Sunday, and thus Shavuot would always be on a Sunday.

Why the difference? Why this seemingly intentional change?

If Judaism interpreted the verses as written in the Hebrew, Firstfruits would always fall on the Sunday during Unleavened Bread, which would be on Resurrection Day, what Christians call Easter Sunday! And Shavuot would always fall on a

Sunday seven weeks later, which would be on the Christian holiday of Pentecost!

So the mis-translations, I believe, are clearly done to keep the Jewish and Christian holidays from being connected in the minds of the Jewish people. This was done by the Jewish translators. So, to me, it's clear that they didn't want the Jewish people to see that Yeshua was fulfilling Jewish Biblical holidays. It's interesting how far they went from what it actually says in the Hebrew, so they wouldn't have to have the embarrassment, if you will, of explaining to their people when they ask questions like, "Well, how come the Christians are celebrating a holiday the same day we're celebrating a holiday?" This way most years the two do not line up.

This also worked to keep Christian scholars from seeing that Christianity is really Jewish because they also wouldn't see that the holidays line up. They would just take the Jewish people's word for it. "Oh, we celebrate on a different day." But I think that in the beginning in Acts, they were both on the exact same day, and what is at work here are spirits of anti-Semitism and spirits of anti-Christ. Anti-Christ spirits are keeping the Jewish people from seeing Yeshua, and anti-Semitic spirits are keeping the Christians from seeing their connection to the Jewish people and their Jewish roots. This really got me when I saw this because it is so clear.

Resurrection Day

So, to review, Yeshua was crucified on which Moad (Appointed Time)? Passover! What significant event in the life of Yeshua happened on the Sunday during the week of Passover? Say it with me, "His Resurrection!" We have lots of Scriptural evidence of this.

> John 20:1 *Early on the first day of the week, while it was still dark, Miryam from Magdala [Mary*

Magdalene] went to the tomb and saw that the stone had been removed from the tomb.

So, it was definitely on the first day of the week. So we see this connection that Yeshua was resurrected on a Biblical Jewish Holiday, just as He was crucified on a Jewish Biblical holiday. He was resurrected on the Biblical holiday of Firstfruits, HaBikkurim.

Some years Firstfruits is on Easter Sunday. Sometimes the calendars align, but not always. But ever since His Resurrection, Yeshua's followers have remembered it on the day following the Sabbath. It has always been on a Sunday.

Here's what we need to see. We need to go back in time and see it. In the first century, all the Jewish followers of Yeshua—all the apostles, all the authors of the New Covenant Scriptures, all the first tens of thousands of believers—would have celebrated His Resurrection and Firstfruits on the same day, on a Sunday. They would have been celebrating Firstfruits according to the Torah commandment. They would've been rejoicing in the first new grain, and they would've been rejoicing in Yeshua having been resurrected.

But, then since the Council of Nicea around 325 CE until recently, there has been no understanding by either group that He was resurrected on Firstfruits, neither the church nor the Jewish community. Since 325, the church has ignored the Moad of Firstfruits. The church celebrates Yeshua's Resurrection, but only that. We Messianic Jews celebrate His Resurrection, along with keeping the Moad, HaBikkurim. As the church does, we do focus on the great display of God's power in resurrecting Yeshua, and the great joy of seeing Him risen from the dead, of Him being still alive today, and His Resurrection being a confirmation that He indeed was sent by God, that He is who He said He is, while also celebrating Him as the Firstfruits..

What has been missing from this Disconnect?

So the question is what has the church been missing because they don't associate the Resurrection with the holiday of Firstfruits? God always has a purpose in putting these special events on certain Moadim. We will see that God chose to resurrect Yeshua on Firstfruits to remind us of something very important for our faith—a foundation stone of our faith, and we don't have to figure this out ourselves because Rabbi Sha'ul (Paul) teaches on the subject.

> 1 Corinthians 15:20 *But the fact is that the Messiah has been raised from the dead, the first-fruits of those who have died.*

(Other translations say, those who have "fallen asleep," which was used to describe what has happened to believers who have eternal life who have physically died.)

> 1 Corinthians 15:21-23a *For since death came through a man, also the resurrection of the dead has come through a man. 22 For just as in connection with Adam all die, so in connection with the Messiah all will be made alive. 23 But each in his own order: the Messiah is the firstfruits;....*

So right here in these four verses, Rabbi Sha'ul has called Messiah the firstfruits. He says it twice. There must be some importance to it because Rabbi Sha'ul is repeating it. Messiah, who rose on the Appointed Time of Firstfruits is twice called the firstfruits. He is the firstfruits of believers who have physically died.

> 1 Corinthians 15:23b *....then those who belong to the Messiah, at the time of his coming....*

"At the time of His coming" refers to His future return, and "those who belong to Him" are those who are in Messiah.

> 1 Corinthians 15:23c *...will all be made alive"*

When Messiah returns, He will resurrect all who "belong to Him."

This is a foundation stone of our faith, our resurrection in the future. Yeshua and His Resurrection is the chief cornerstone, but our future resurrection to be with Him is part of the foundation. So I believe this is why God has put these two things together so that we would be reminded of this every year. God arranged this timing to strengthen our faith in our future bodily resurrection. By Resurrection Day falling on Firstfruits, we are reminded that Yeshua is the Firstfruits of those believers who will rise from the dead, that we are going to be resurrected, that there is going to be this great harvest of souls. And who will that harvest be? Well, I hope it is going to be you! I know it is going to be me.

So to re-cap, Yeshua was offered as a firstfruits offering by His Father in expectation that a bountiful harvest would follow. God planned for us to remember every year that His resurrection was the firstfruits of the coming harvest of resurrected souls. Yeshua's resurrection happened on Firstfruits to strengthen your faith that after you die, you will rise again to be forever with Him. (More on this later.)

Chapter 2
MYSTERIES OF THE TORN CURTAIN*

Resurrection and Firstfruits Review

The book of Hebrews tells us that a new and living way was opened through the parokhet, the curtain into the Holy of Holies that allows all the followers of Yeshua to enter the presence of God.

> Hebrews 10:19-20 *So, brothers, we have confidence to use the way into the Holiest Place opened by the blood of Yeshua. 20 He inaugurated it for us as a new and living way through the parokhet [the curtain between the Holy Place and the Most Holy Place in the Temple] by means of his flesh.*

Yeshua's Resurrection is God's confirmation that Yeshua's Crucifixion was for a purpose. Just as the Bible records that Yeshua <u>died</u> on the exact day of the Biblical Moad of Pesakh (Passover), it also records He was resurrected on

---

* This chapter is similar to chapters 6 and 7 of my book, *Yom Kippur, The Day of Atonement*, but it is so good that even if you have already read my *Yom Kippur* book, it is worth a review.

the Sunday after the Shabbat during the Pesakh week which is another Biblical Appointed Time - Yom HaBikkurim, the Day of Firstfruits. As we pointed out in the last chapter, Rabbi Sha'ul refers to this connection.

> 1 Corinthians 15:20 *But the fact is that the Messiah has been raised from the dead, the first-fruits of those who have died.*

Why would God choose this Moad of Firstfruits for Yeshua's Resurrection? Well, again, I think the most obvious reason is to remind us that He is the Firstfruits of the great resurrection of all people. Right? There will be a day when all people will be resurrected.

> Daniel 12:2 *And multitudes of those who sleep in the dust of the earth shall awake, some to everlasting life, some to shame and everlasting contempt.*

Those who don't trust in Yeshua will be resurrected to face judgment and will be ashamed of how that judgment comes out. It is not something to look forward to. Those who trust in Yeshua will be resurrected to everlasting life. We have this great hope to look forward to. When you have a firstfruit, it means there will be second and third fruits or latter fruits. He is the firstfruit of the Resurrection, we are the latter fruits of the Resurrection, which we are reminded of each year as we remember that Yeshua's resurrection happened on Firstfruits. Living with this hope makes life very different. The struggles of this life don't seem as important.

The Curtain

In this chapter and the next one, we want to look at what happened between Yeshua's Crucifixion and Resurrection. In this chapter we will focus on the first thing, the curtain tearing. What the Spirit of God showed me is that there are eight important meanings to us today of that one specific, significant event that happened first during this time. This was revealed to me as I tried to solve a mystery in the Scriptures, trying to understand what this was about.

So where we're going to go is take ourselves back to the Hill of Golgotha where Yeshua is on the Cross. After several hours on the Cross, right at the end, Yeshua gave His life for us.

> Matthew 27:50-51 *But Yeshua, again crying out in a loud voice, yielded up his spirit. 51 At that moment the parokhet (the curtain) in the Temple was ripped in two from top to bottom; and there was an earthquake, with rocks splitting apart.*

The mystery is, why was this parokhet (curtain) ripped in two from the top to the bottom? The ripping of this curtain and Matthew's statements "at that moment" and "top to bottom" are some of the clues that led me to the eight meanings of this mysterious event. Really, some of these meanings are profound and amazing to me. Let's look at these clues.

So first we have the statement, "at that moment." What moment was it? It was the exact instant of Yeshua's death. It means the very moment His sacrifice was completed on the Cross.

Then we have the curtain being ripped from "top to bottom." To understand this, we need to understand the function of this curtain in the Temple. The curtain was hung over the entrance to the Holiest Place, the Holy of Holies. It was in the Temple in Jerusalem for 1500 years until 70 CE when the Temple was destroyed.

Slide of curtain

The curtain was blue and red. It hung from ceiling to floor and was very thick. It was decorated with cherubim (Ex.

26:31). It separated the Holy Place from the most Holy Place where the Aron Brit, the Ark of the Covenant was located. The cover of the Ark was called the Kapporet, the Mercy Seat. It was the throne of God on earth where God appeared to the Israelites.

The curtain separated the people, including the cohanim, the priests, from the manifest presence of God. When I say "manifest presence," I mean His presence in a way that human beings can observe it, like when He manifested as the pillar of fire and cloud in the desert.

Once a year on Yom Kippur, the Day of Atonement, the Levitical Cohane HaGadol, the High Priest went alone through the curtain into the Holiest Place. Since it was a single curtain, he must have pushed it aside to enter. He was required by God's commandments to be dressed in a special white garment, and he had to carry with Him a bowl of the blood of the sacrificed animals to sprinkle on the Kapporet, the Mercy Seat on top of the Aron Brit, Ark of the Covenant. The blood made atonement for the sin of the entire nation of Israel for the past year. This atoning sacrifice enabled the presence of the Holy God to dwell in the Temple in the midst of them. This ceremony was repeated every year on Yom Kippur.

His Presence Consumes

Why was this blood atonement needed? One of God's primary characteristics is that He is holy – kadosh. The Hebrew word means set apart, separate. It signifies He is separate from evil. So, God cannot dwell among a sinful people. It's not just that God would be uncomfortable in the presence of sin. It's that sin, and whatever container it's in, burns up in His presence. So the manifest presence of God that dwelt over the Mercy Seat would have destroyed the people without the atonement because of the sinful nature in them which is also in us. Read Exodus 33, especially verse 5 to understand this.

> Exodus 33:5 *Adonai said to Moses, "Say to Bnei-Yisrael, 'You are a stiff-necked people. If I were going up among you for one moment, I would consume you....*

He would consume them. The holy power of His presence would be too much for sinful humans to be near. How does this apply to us today? No one, including me, has ever lived their life without violating God's laws, and because we violated God's laws, our destiny should be the eternal fires of hell rather than Heaven where we could be eternally in God's powerful, holy presence.

In the time of the Temple, because of the Yom Kippur atonement and the other atoning blood sacrifices, people's sin could be atoned for—covered, and they could be forgiven and come into His presence. But, the Temple was destroyed in 70 CE and sacrifices have not been made since its destruction. But God did not leave people without a way of atoning for sin, so we can come into His presence.

He put His plan into place 37 years before the Temple's destruction. He came to earth in the form of a man, Yeshua HaMashiakih, the Messiah. He was falsely accused and allowed Himself to be executed on the Cross as the final sacrifice, and rose from the dead to demonstrate that His sacrifice was God's plan for our salvation. He wasn't a lunatic making false claims as some in His day thought, and some today still believe. He was God's only begotten Son, Emanu-El, God with us, HaShem Himself come in the flesh, who did everything according to God's plan for our salvation.

The First Meaning, Once and For All

Then, we read that as He died, the curtain in the Temple was torn in two. So, what's the meaning of this? Well, the author of Hebrews gives the first meaning of this very clearly.

> Hebrews 9:11 (TLV) *But when Messiah appeared as Kohen Gadol [High Priest] of the good things that have now come, passing through the greater and more perfect Tent [Tabernacle] not made with hands (that is to say not of this creation),*

That is, it is not of this created world.

> Hebrews 9:12 (TLV) *He entered into the Holies once for all—not by the blood of goats and calves but by His own blood, having obtained eternal redemption.*

> Hebrew 9:12 (NKJV) *Not with the blood of goats and calves, but with His own blood He entered the Most Holy Place once for all, having obtained eternal redemption.*

The amazing dual role of the Messiah is described here, being both the sacrifice and our Great High Priest, our Cohane HaGadol! He brought His own Blood as the full and final sacrifice. Yes, you can praise the Lord right now for that! Hallelujah!!! Thank You, Yeshua!!

Now where is the "greater and more perfect Tabernacle" He entered? It's God's throne-room in Heaven. The Temple in Jerusalem was a model of this more perfect Tabernacle, built according to what God showed to Moses on Mt. Sinai.

So Yeshua made a sacrifice similar to the ones made on Yom Kippur in the Temple, but, He did it in the real Holiest Place, the throne of God in Heaven. What did Yeshua bring with Him into that Most Holy Place in Heaven? Not the blood of sacrificed animals. He carried His own Blood, the Blood of the Lamb of God. He offered His own Blood on the throne of

God rather than the earthly Mercy Seat. He sprinkled it on the real throne of God in the real Tabernacle in Heaven.

What power did this offering of His Blood have?

> Hebrews 9:13 *For if sprinkling ceremonially unclean persons with the blood of goats and bulls and the ashes of a heifer restores their outward purity;*

This is referring to purification ceremonies in the Temple on earth.

> Hebrews 9:14 *then how much more the blood of the Messiah, who, through the eternal Spirit, offered himself to God as a sacrifice without blemish, will purify our conscience from works that lead to death, so that we can serve the living God!*

How much more effective is this offering of the Blood of the Son of God than the offerings of the blood of animals? Those offerings had to be repeated year after year but:

> Hebrews 9:12 *he entered the Holiest Place once and for all*

The Yom Kippur atoning sacrifice had to be made yearly, but Yeshua's sacrifice was once and for all. It never has to be repeated. It dealt with all sin, for all time, for all people. The curtain was torn in two rather than pushed aside. If it had been pushed aside and not torn, it would have meant the sacrifice would have had to be repeated every year. So the first meaning of the mystery of the torn curtain is that Yeshua's sacrifice is forever!

The Second Meaning, Confidence

> Hebrews 10:19-20 *So, brothers, we have confidence to use the way into the Holiest Place opened by the blood of Yeshua. 20 He inaugurated it for us as a new and living way through the curtain, by means of his flesh*

What else did the tearing of the curtain in the Temple signify? If we have received His atoning sacrifice, we can have "confidence to use the way into the Holiest Place" to be in the presence of God without being consumed by coming too close to the Holy God. It's not just for the High Priest once a year anymore. It is open to all who would come. We can enter boldly with confidence! The second meaning of the torn curtain is we have confidence to come boldly before the throne of God! So, if you are struggling and the enemy is telling you that because of your sin, failure, foolishness, etc. God isn't going to hear your prayers, you can tell him that you can come confidently into God's presence because Yeshua opened the way.

The Third Meaning, The Way is Opened

The torn curtain means the way has been opened for people to come into God's presence.

> Matthew 27:51 *At that moment the parokhet in the Temple was ripped in two from top to bottom; and there was an earthquake, with rocks splitting apart.*

How did Matthew know it was torn from top to bottom? He could only have written this if there had been a witness. Who was present while it was being torn? It had to be one or more priests because only priests were allowed into the Holy Place in front of the curtain.

Why was it torn from top to bottom? Because God did it, not man. No man could open the way to God. The third meaning of the torn curtain is that the way is opened to enter to be with God. It was opened by Yeshua, by God because no human being could tear the *parokhet* from top to bottom.

The Fourth Meaning, Invited

It was a sovereign act of God to invite you and I to come into His presence. When you need to be confident that you can come into His presence and He will hear you, remember, the curtain was not torn from bottom to top. It's been torn from top to bottom because God made the way.

> Hebrews 4:16 *Therefore, let us <u>confidently</u> approach the throne from which God gives grace, so that we may receive mercy and find grace in our time of need.*

God wants your faith to be strengthened that you can approach Him and His throne of grace with confidence. I don't know about you, but for me in times when I've been struggling in prayer, and my faith level is low, I remember I'm supposed to come confidently to His throne because He ripped the *parokhet*, the separating curtain. He is inviting me to come in. He'll never reject me when I come. <u>The fourth meaning of the torn curtain is we are invited to come.</u>

The Fifth Meaning, His Body

> Hebrews 10:20 *He inaugurated it for us as a new and living way through <u>the curtain, by means of his flesh.</u>*

> NKJV: *a new and living way through the curtain, that is, His Body*

The literal translation of the Greek is "through the curtain, this is of the flesh of Him." So what does this mean? What is the significance of the phrase, "a new and living way through the curtain, that is, His body"? I saw two possible answers, and I believe both of them are valid, and have practical applications to our lives. So hang on with me here and focus because you're going to love this when you get it, but it's going to take some concentration. Okay?

The first answer agrees with what we just discussed. "That is, his body" refers to the actual way through the curtain. By offering His Body, Yeshua opened a way through the curtain for us. The offering of His body tore the curtain in two. It's like, as He was dying, God took that curtain in His hands and just ripped it. So that's the first answer. It is pretty straight forward.

The second answer is "a new and living way through the curtain that is, his body." Can we see a different way of understanding that? Here's where you have to focus on, the curtain that is, his body." What I saw was His Body is being referred to as being the curtain. Do you see that? So this sent me off studying. In what way was Yeshua's body the curtain that was torn, that there was a new and living way through? Well, referring to Yeshua, Paul writes:

> Colossians 2:9 *For in Him dwells all the fullness of the Godhead bodily;*

So here's what came to me, and I just pray you'll get this. When Yeshua walked this earth, the fullness of God dwelt in His body. Do you agree with that? So, His human flesh was like a curtain concealing the fullness of God dwelling inside Him. Do you see that? So, if His body was the curtain, how was "a new and living way" opened through His body?

> Isaiah 53:5 *But He was wounded for our trans-gressions,...*

The Hebrew word for *"wounded"* is *"chalal,"* which means breaking the skin. So His skin, the curtain that concealed His divine nature, was torn open by the Roman soldier's whip, by the crown of thorns, by the nails, and by the spear. So, His skin was torn just like the curtain in the Temple was torn.

Now, so that you don't think this is wild and that I am making this up, let's look a little later at the description of what happened on the Cross when the "new and living way through the curtain, that is, His body" was opened up. Let's read a few verses further in Matthew's description of what happened after Yeshua yielded up His Spirit and the curtain was torn in two. Listen to this.

> Matthew 27:54 *When the Roman officer and those who were with him who were keeping watch over Yeshua saw the earthquake and what was happening they were awestruck and said, "He is really the Son of God."*

What happened to these Roman soldiers when the earthquake shook the ground at the moment Messiah died? They became convinced that Yeshua was the Son of God. And Yeshua said:

> John 14:9... *Anyone who has seen me has seen the Father.*

So in seeing that Yeshua was actually the Son of God, these soldiers were seeing the presence of God. They were seeing through Yeshua's human flesh to the Truth that Yeshua and God are one and God was in Him. Let me say that again. They saw through Yeshua's flesh that was concealing God in Him to God in Him. They saw that Yeshua and God are One, and they confessed it. They called Him the Son of God. So the Roman soldiers saw through this "new and living way opened for us through the curtain—His body!" Are you grasping this? They saw through the curtain of His skin to what was inside—God Himself. They entered the presence of God through the new and living way, the torn flesh of the Messiah by believing that He is the Son of God.

This happened to me years ago when I first started reading the Bible. I'd heard about Yeshua that He was a great man, that He said and did great things. But I never understood who He was or why He was so important. One day, at a moment of great crisis, I asked Him for help. It was the first time I ever did that and He helped me in a miraculous way. Suddenly, it was like my eyes were opened. I saw Him for who He really was, that He was God come as a man. I saw through His human body, like it was a parted curtain to the manifest presence of God living within His flesh. Then I was able to come into God's presence through that "new and living way through the curtain, by means of His flesh."

What happened to me may be similar to what happened to you. You were able to see He was God Himself come as a man and that sight enabled you to come into God's presence, into His Kingdom. So the fifth meaning is that the torn curtain is His body.

The Sixth Meaning, The Timing

The curtain that was torn was the curtain of Yeshua's skin, flesh, body so that people could see God dwelling inside Him and come to Him as their Savior and Lord, their God. The curtain was torn as Yeshua entered God's throne room, the Holiest Place in Heaven. We know He sprinkled His Blood there at that moment. It didn't take long, just a moment to do it. Sprinkling His blood on God's throne was the action that brought Redemption to the world. It was the greatest thing that God has ever done for us. It was the turning point of the history of this planet and perhaps of all life.

There's another powerful meaning in the mystery of His timing of this act. It didn't happen after His Resurrection, after He arose and appeared to His disciples. It happened before He appeared to His disciples. It happened at the moment of His death on the Cross. To His disciples this was the moment of greatest despair. At that moment, the great hope they had in Him was completely destroyed. They were utterly without hope. They were hiding from the Romans. They were sure Yeshua had failed. They were ashamed of how they had deserted Him when facing His arrest. Yet at that very moment, God achieved His greatest victory—atonement for the whole world for all time.

What does this say to us?

It means we need to persevere. We need to hold on to our hope, our faith. It is especially when situations look the worst that God may be doing great things that are invisible to us. Some of you reading this book may be without hope over something important to you. How do you know God isn't doing a miracle right now that you can't see? <u>The sixth meaning of the torn curtain is about the timing. At the disciples moment of greatest despair, God did the greatest, most miraculous thing ever for us.</u>

The Seventh Meaning, Our Flesh

Let's go back to the fifth meaning of the torn curtain to see the seventh meaning. The curtain that was torn was Yeshua's torn flesh. People can now see through the torn curtain of Yeshua's flesh to who Yeshua really is, God come as a man. There's another very important application of this mystery. Yeshua says He Himself dwells in His followers, in me and in each of you.

> John 14:20 At that day you will know that I am in My Father, and you in Me, and I in you.

God is dwelling in me, but you can't see Him with your natural eyes. In the Spirit you may be able to see Him. If you observe me doing Godly things, you may be able to see Him in me. But, if you observe me behaving in a carnal, sinful way, He will be hidden. So my carnal nature, my old man can be a curtain concealing God from others.

The same is true for your flesh, your carnal nature, your old man. It can keep others from seeing God in you.

So your flesh, your carnal nature may be keeping other people from seeing God in you. When you walk in the Spirit, other people can see through your flesh to God's presence in you. Do you know someone you can see Yeshua in? That person has been crucifying their own flesh, their carnal nature, enabling Yeshua's nature, His Spirit, and His Life to be seen through them. So the <u>seventh meaning of the mystery of the torn curtain is that your actions and attitudes might be hiding Yeshua from people.</u>

The Eighth Meaning, The Corporate Body

I see Yeshua in my congregants. The Ruakh HaKodesh dwells in each of us individually, but also in us altogether, corporately, as the Body of Messiah. The ungodly behavior of His Body is also like a curtain concealing Him from others.

People are supposed to be able to see through the curtain of the Body of Messiah to the manifest presence of God filling His people corporately. But so many times because of what the "Body" the church is or has been doing, the curtain is dark and thick. This is the curtain, the veil that has kept our Jewish people from seeing Him. Rabbi Sha'ul was writing about the Jewish people of His day.

> 2 Corinthians 3:15 *Yes, till today, whenever Moshe is read, a veil lies over their heart.*

Today the veil over Jewish hearts is due to the centuries of conflict between the church and the Jewish people. The church today has cut itself off from its Jewish Roots, so Christians don't appear to Jewish people to be worshipping the God of Israel. The fear, distrust, and bitterness of that conflict and the confusion and deception of replacement theology have created a veil keeping Jewish people from seeing the God of Israel in the church. My life's goal is to see that veil torn because God's full plan for the world won't be complete until the veil over Jewish hearts is torn and they see Yeshua as the Messiah. <u>The eighth meaning of the torn curtain is that the sin of the corporate Body of Messiah can be a curtain blocking the view of people, especially the Jewish people from seeing Yeshua.</u>

Let's pray

Yeshua, we remember with thanksgiving what You did during this season, dying on the Cross to pay the price for our sin, sprinkling Your Blood on the altar in Heaven, rising from the dead to confirm Your victory.

Help us to live with the hope that You are the Firstfruits of the Resurrection, and we who have put our trust in You as Messiah are the latter fruits and will be resurrected someday to eternal life.

Thank You for this amazing phrase in Your Word, "a new and living way through the curtain, that is His flesh." Give all of us confidence that we can come into Your presence because You went through that curtain in Heaven for us and ripped the curtain on earth to show us that we could follow You, and come into Your presence.

Thank You that You didn't push it aside, You ripped it to show us that Your atonement was for all sin, for all time. Thank you that You ripped it from top to bottom to show us that You, God, were the one pouring out Your grace to bring us to You.

Thank you that You ripped that veil when the world was at its darkest moment, when all hope was gone to show us that when walking with You, we should have hope in the worst of circumstances.

Enable us to see that You live within each of us and that our flesh conceals Your Spirit from others. Help us to crucify our flesh daily that others may see You in us.

Enable us to see that You live in us as a corporate Body. Help us to function together as a Body that others may see You in us. Rip the veil over the hearts of Jewish people so they can see through to the truth that You are the Messiah of Israel.

Thank you that you ripped the veil of the flesh of the Son of God so that we could see through to God dwelling inside Him. In the mighty, all-powerful Name of Yeshua, we pray. Amen

*****

If you have never seen through the veil that is His flesh, God wants to give you spiritual eyes to see God through Yeshua's torn flesh. If you are seeing Him today for the first time and want to come to Him to be His child and avoid the punishment of hell, pray with me.

I recognize I have broken Your Laws, God. I take responsibility for my disobedience. Forgive me in Yeshua's Name. I put my trust in Your sacrificial death on the Cross to pay the penalty for my sins. I receive Your forgiveness. I believe You rose from the dead to confirm that Your sacrifice was real. I submit myself to You as my Lord. Take charge of my life and lead me. I will obey Your Word. In Yeshua's Name I pray. Amen.

Chapter 3

BETWEEN THE CROSS AND RESURRECTION

People Came Out Of Their Tombs

There's another connection between Yeshua's Resurrection and Firstfruits in the Bible that reinforces that He is the Firstfruits. I recently saw the application of this and why it is so important. Maybe you have never seen this before. Maybe you have. Here's what this is about. Referring to the moment of Yeshua's death on the Cross, Matthew says this:

> Matthew 27:51 *At that moment the parokhet [the curtain into the Most Holy Place] in the Temple was ripped in two from top to bottom; and there was an earthquake, with rocks splitting apart.*

We just studied the meaning of the curtain ripping, so let's move on and look at what the next verse says.

> Matthew 27:52 *Also the graves were opened, and the bodies of many holy people who had died were raised to life;*

Understand that the tombs back then were generally caves carved in rocks or were naturally occurring caves, and they had large stones covering the entrances. So, an earthquake would have opened these tombs. It wasn't like you had someone buried deep in the ground in a coffin that wouldn't so likely be uncovered in an earthquake. I guess it could happen. The earth could open up in deep cracks and the coffin could be thrown up out of a crack or something like that. But for cave-like tombs, the stones could pretty easily be shaken away from the openings by an earthquake. Notice that it says there were many holy people who were resurrected. Then verse 53 says this.

> Matthew 27:53 *and after Yeshua rose, they came out of the graves and went into the holy city, where many people saw them.*

This is something that I had never really thought about before. It was revealed to me as I was studying for Firstfruits one year. It is really an amazing thing. It uses the word "many" a couple times. And it doesn't give us much more information. None of the other Gospels speak about it, but it happened.

Right away, I saw some confusion here that I want to try to clear up. I hope you can follow me.

As you read through this, it sounds like the tombs were opened and these dead holy people came to life at the time Yeshua was crucified. Right? But then it sounds like they remained in their open tombs for three days until after Yeshua rose from the dead, and then they appeared. Do you see that? It's because it puts the time that they came alive at the same time as when the curtain was ripped. That happened when He died, which was three days before He arose. It says they appeared after He arose.

Do you see the confusion there? It is a little strange, and there really isn't any other explanation of it. So you can take this or leave it, but here is how I understood it. So basically, the verse is saying, "After Yeshua's resurrection, they came out and went into the city of Jerusalem where they were seen by many people."

The timing should be understood that the tombs were opened by the earthquake when Yeshua died. Then when He rose, that's when these holy people came to life. Then they came out of the tombs and went into city where they were seen by many. Why is the timing important? Well, if they arose before Yeshua arose, then He wouldn't be the Firstfruits. Right? And they wouldn't have risen on Firstfruits. They would have risen before Firstfruits.

We really just have to guess at this since it is only written about here in Matthew, but I think I see you nodding that you agree with me.

******

Now, just take a moment and imagine with me what it would have been like for the people in that day with all these very strange things happening within days of each other. While Yeshua of Nazareth was crucified, it got dark for three hours at midday. When He died, there was an earthquake. Some of the damage was that tombs were opened, which caused apprehension because they are all trying to stay purified for Pesakh. Then the news came out that the huge, thick curtain in the Temple was ripped from top to bottom!

This all happened while they were trying to prepare for their second Seder. [If they loved Yeshua, they were also mourning His death and were angry at their leaders for arresting Him, and were in shock that this happened to Him because they thought He was the Messiah.]

Then just three days later when they were up early getting their baskets of Firstfruits offerings ready for going in the processional to the Temple, there was another earthquake!

Then something very disturbing happened. Some people long dead, whose bodies should have been totally decayed, appeared in the city, shocking everyone to the core. Then came the "official" news that Yeshua's body was stolen! But other "unofficial" news spread that He was seen alive by His followers! Wow! What a whirl wind, torrent of emotions those people were going through! And all of it happening on special Moadim! God was shaking them up, preparing them to be ready to believe in Yeshua!

*****

Okay, back to the holy people who came to life. Another question that came to my mind is, what kind of bodies did these holy people have? I was thinking about that and I thought, you know, it doesn't sound like they were people who just died a couple days before, like Lazarus died and was in the grave only four days before he was raised. But for these people, the bodies they lived in on earth probably were decayed. I believe they came out of those graves with new, resurrected bodies that God gave them, based somehow, I don't know, maybe on the DNA of their old, decayed bodies?

So, who were these holy people? Here's my understanding, gleaned from the Bible. Yeshua spoke about a righteous beggar named Lazarus.

> Luke 16:22 *In time the beggar died and was carried away by the angels to Avraham's side* [in other translations, *"bosom"*]; ...

From the rest of the account, we learn that this was a good place where people were waiting for what Rabbi Sha'ul (Paul) describes in Ephesians, when speaking of Messiah.

> Ephesians 4:8 *This is why it says, "After he went up into the heights, he led captivity captive and he gave gifts to mankind." 9 Now this phrase, "he went up," what can it mean if not that he first went down into the lower parts, that is, the earth?*

So I understand that these holy people who rose with Yeshua had been with Lazarus in Abraham's bosom. They were not in Heaven but in the lower parts of the earth. After His Crucifixion, Yeshua went down to them and led those who had been waiting in Abraham's bosom into Heaven to be in the presence of God. And according to the Scripture, we read, there were many of them, and they were seen by many people.

So, who were they? Well, it says they were holy people. I believe they were Old Testament or Tanakh saints and saints from the years in between the two Covenant Scriptures. There are some we can be sure of, and some we are not sure of. We can be sure that it could have been some of these: Enoch, Noah, Avraham, Sarah, Yosef, Moses, David, Isaiah, Jeremiah, Ezekiel, Daniel and a whole bunch of others that might have also been risen at this time. There were also people in Yeshua's time that were righteous that it could've been, like Yeshua's adopted father, Joseph, and Zechariah, the father of Yochanan, the immerser (John the Baptist) and his wife Elizabeth. How about Simeon who met baby Yeshua in the Temple, and Anna who prophesied there, and Yochanan the immerser, himself, too. Where were they? When did they get to Heaven? Well, maybe not until after Yeshua's sacrifice and Resurrection.

But here's another question. Did those who came to life live for a few years and then die again maybe when they got to be 100 years old or older? Do you think so? I don't, because if they had, we would surely have some testimonies from them. Surely there would be something written about them. So, again, when did they go to Heaven? How long did they hang around?

Well, we concluded that they came to life after Yeshua's bodily resurrection. Right? Well, since Yeshua is the Firstfruits,

He would have been the first to rise from dead bodily. So they had to have risen after He arose. So Yeshua was the first to go into Heaven in a resurrected body. So they would have had to wait until after that also.

He Went To Heaven Three Times

Now, I hope I don't lose you here. I understand that Yeshua went to Heaven three times. Okay? He went once in the Spirit and twice in His body. I see a questioning look on your face, like What? Let me explain.

The first time in the Spirit was at the moment of His death on the Cross.

> Hebrews 9:11-12 *But when the Messiah appeared as cohen gadol [high priest] of the good things that are happening already, then, through the greater and more perfect Tent (Tabernacle) which is not man-made (that is, it is not of this created world), 12 he entered the Holiest Place once and for all. And he entered not by means of the blood of goats and calves, but by means of his own blood, thus setting people free forever.*

> Hebrew 9:12 (NKJV) *Not with the blood of goats and calves, but with His own blood He entered the Most Holy Place once for all, having obtained eternal redemption.*

So His blood was poured out on the Cross, and that opened the way for Him to enter the more perfect Tent, which is the Holiest Place in Heaven. He didn't enter in bodily form because He hadn't resurrected yet. That was three days later. Do you see that? This was new to me. I was like, "Oh, He must have done that before He was resurrected." It was when the parokhet/curtain was torn. When was it torn? Yes, at the moment of His death. Right? Not at His Resurrection, but at the moment He died, which signified that the way was opened into Holy of Holies or Holiest Place. Do you follow me so far?

Then, here's what I believe happened after that. For three days in the Spirit, His body still not resurrected, He was in the depths of the earth, warring in the Spirit against satan.

> Colossians 2:13b-15 (TLV) *God made you alive together with Him when He pardoned us all our transgressions. 14 He wiped out the handwritten record of debts with the decrees against us, which was hostile to us. He took it away by nailing it to the cross. 15 After disarming the principalities and powers, He made a public spectacle of them, triumphing over them in the cross*

And He preached the Gospel to the people who died in the flood.

> I Peter 3:18-20 *For the Messiah himself died for sins, once and for all, a righteous person on behalf of unrighteous people, so that he might bring you to God. He was put to death in the flesh but brought to life by the Spirit; 19 and in this form he went and made a proclamation to the imprisoned spirits, 20 to those who were disobedient long ago, in the days of Noach, when God waited patiently during the building of the ark,.*

Then on the third day He arose in bodily form. We'll read that He went to Heaven again in John 20. Then we all know that 40 days later, as Acts 1 tells us, His body ascended to Heaven for the second time. So He went to Heaven three times, once in the Spirit and two times in His body.

Let's look at that initial bodily ascent, on the day He rose again in John 20. It was early on the morning of the day of His resurrection, on Firstfruits. Miryam was at His tomb, which was an open and empty tomb, and suddenly He appeared to her. He spoke her name, and she recognized Him. She knelt in worship. Then here's where I got the clue to all this body stuff. What did she do next? She grasped His feet. He had a body, okay? And she grabbed His feet. This is where we find out what happened to that body.

> John 20:17 *"Stop holding onto me," Yeshua said to her, "because I haven't yet gone back to the Father. But go to my brothers, and tell them that I am going back to my Father and your Father, to my God and your God."*

So, she was holding on to His feet, meaning He had a physical body. He had resurrected in physical form at this point. And He is saying here that He was about to ascend in that body to the Father. Do you follow that?

Then, later in that same day, He appeared to two disciples on the road to Emmaus. Then He appeared to the twelve in bodily form because He said, "Touch me and see." And he ate. So He must have come back from the Father before that. Then He was with the disciples for 40 days until His final bodily ascent in Acts 1.

So I believe that it must have been at His first ascent in His resurrected body into Heaven that He brought these "many holy people" with Him to Heaven because I don't think they were there for the 40 days. Or it was somewhere in between there. So here's how I understand this. These holy people were around for only a short time, from time of His resurrection early Sunday morning until after He met Miryam when He actually went up into Heaven in His resurrected body.

*****

So on the next page is a list[8] of my understanding of the sequence of events:

---

8 Also see it in Appendix B at the end of this book.

The Chronological Order of the Death and Resurrection Events

1. Yeshua was crucified and died mid-afternoon on Thursday. His blood was poured out on the Cross, which was the final sacrifice. (See my book, *Pesakh,* and chapter 4 in this book for an explanation of why Thursday and not Friday, as the church has taught.)

2. At the moment of His death, His soul and spirit went to be with God in Heaven where He entered the Holy of Holies.

3. At that same moment, the parokhet/curtain was torn, signifying the way was opened into the Holy of Holies.

4. At that same moment, an earthquake opened the tombs of the righteous.

5. Then He came back and descended into hell, defeated hell and death, and took the keys.

6. Using the keys, He opened the doors of Avraham's bosom.

7. Then His body was resurrected early Sunday morning. Why? Because the prophesy said He had to be in the tomb how long? For 3 days and 3 nights. So it couldn't have happened until after that third night.

8. Many holy people bodily resurrected after Yeshua's bodily Resurrection

9. They went into Jerusalem and were seen by many.

10. Miryam encountered Yeshua and physically touched His resurrected Body, but He told her not to hold onto Him because He had not yet gone to His Father (in His resurrected body).

11. Yeshua ascended to Heaven bodily for the first time.

12. As He ascended (or it could've been later), Yeshua
    brought the people from Avraham's bosom
    with Him into Heaven, including those who had
    resurrected and appeared in the city, and those
    from the flood who heard His Gospel message and
    accepted His atonement (1 Peter 3:18-20).

So that's my take on the chronological order. (It is also listed at the end of this book in Appendix B.) You can study it out yourself and see. Like I said, there is a lot of speculation about this. My understanding is just based on gleaning from the few minor details we are given in the Scripture. (I will discuss it a little more in chapter 4.)

Yeshua Fulfilled Every Detail of Firstfruits

But here is what we do need to know. How should this account of these holy people effect each of us today? Why is that in there? Why did God cause these people to be resurrected? You know that nothing is recorded in Scripture without a reason. There is always a reason for everything. Why were they resurrected and revealed to people?

Well, I see two reasons. The first reason this account of these holy people is given is to strengthen our faith in the prophetic accuracy of God's timing and plan.

When the first grain was offered to the priests, it was an omer, right? Is an omer one grain? No. It was more than a single grain of barley. It was a sheaf with many stalks of grains. So, the firstfruits of those risen from the dead were Yeshua plus those holy people who came out of their graves. Do you see that?

So there was a whole sheaf of resurrections. If it had been just Yeshua, He really would not have fulfilled the commandment to offer a sheaf of barley, having a significant number of grains. God didn't say to offer one grain or one stalk. They were supposed to take several stalks bunched together. That's what was shaken off and put in the omer container.

So it should really strengthen our faith to see this amazing confirmation and fulfillment of this prophetic Appointed Time by Yeshua Himself being the Firstfruit offering. And then of Yeshua turning around and obeying the commandment by bringing an omer of resurrections as His Firstfruit offering in Heaven. As we are learning and delving deep into all the Moadim, we are seeing that Yeshua always obeyed everything. And when He fulfills them, He fulfills every tiny detail. That really blesses my soul. I hope it blesses you also.

We Will Be Part Of The Full Resurrection Harvest

The second reason has to do with what we already mentioned about how when Messiah returns, He will bodily resurrect all who "belong to Him." We are supposed to believe that if we die physically before the Lord returns, we will be resurrected and rise to meet the Lord in the air. Right? Now, I don't know about you. Maybe this is just me. I don't have much trouble believing that Yeshua rose from the dead. I mean you can't even be saved unless you believe that. Right? I mean, the tomb was empty. There were witnesses to it. People saw Him and touched Him. Rabbi Sha'ul says in I Corinthians that actually five hundred saw Him alive after He was crucified, and many of them were still alive when he wrote 1 Corinthians, so they could've contradicted him.

On top of that, Yeshua was God Himself come as a man, right? So why wouldn't that be possible for Him to rise from the dead? He was born of a virgin. In fact, He resurrected at least two dead people Himself, the widow's son and Lazarus. So it is pretty easy to believe that and accept it. Right? But I struggle a little more with believing that I will rise bodily from the dead. How about you? Is it hard for you to believe that your body could be resurrected? I mean, there's no account of the apostles being resurrected. I myself haven't seen anyone raised from the dead. Have you?

We know that when people die physically, their bodies decay. They rot in the grave. Some people even choose cremation. They are just reduced to ashes. So it's a little harder to believe that our bodies will be resurrected. Here's the real test. What happens when you are in a situation where you could lose your life? Are you in the place where you can say, "I know where I'm going. I will be resurrected. It's easy for me." It's easy to say that until it actually happens, right? Then it becomes a little harder.

So I believe this account of the many holy people who were physically risen from the dead was given to us to strengthen our faith, to strengthen your faith that you too will rise from dead, because they were ordinary people who were resurrected. It says they were holy people, but we are holy people, too, by the Blood of Yeshua. They weren't divine. They were just people. If you read some of their accounts, they had struggles just like us. Look at Abraham. He struggled. He had some sin in his life. And David! He committed some terrible sins, but he repented and was forgiven. They weren't perfect people, but they were resurrected.

So let's just look at some verses to strengthen our faith just a little more because that's the whole purpose of this, to encourage your faith. The Bible speaks of a gathering of souls on the Day of the Lord as a great harvest.

> Matthew 24:30-31 "Then the sign of the Son
> of Man will appear in the sky, all the tribes of
> the Land will mourn, and they will see the Son
> of Man coming on the clouds of heaven with
> tremendous power and glory. 31 He will send
> out his angels with a great shofar; and they will

gather together his chosen people from the four
winds, from one end of heaven to the other."

This is the resurrection harvest. The Firstfruits has already
been harvested. This is the great harvest that is coming.
Rabbi Sha'ul adds to that teaching in Matthew, dealing with
people who will still be alive at the time of Yeshua's coming
and those who have died before He comes.

> 1 Thessalonians 4:15-17 ...we who remain
> alive when the Lord comes will certainly not
> take precedence over those who have died.
> 16 For the Lord himself will come down from
> heaven with a rousing cry, with a call from one
> of the ruling angels, and with God's shofar
> [trumpet]; those who died united with [in] the
> Messiah will be the first to rise; 17 then we who
> are left still alive will be caught up with them in
> the clouds to meet the Lord in the air; and thus
> we will always be with the Lord.

This is pretty wild. I mean, this is really radical what he
is saying here. This will be not just people who are alive at
the time, but people will come out of their graves. I'm sure
you have heard it referred to as the rapture, but literally, it
will be millions of people who are in their graves who will
be resurrected and will join those of us who are alive—I'm
hoping I will still be alive—and altogether we are going to rise
up to meet Him into the air. I can't even imagine what this is
going to be like. There have been lots of films made trying to
imagine what's going to happens when airplane pilots and
bus drivers suddenly disappear. Who knows?

This is going to be that time when the second fruits or the
latter fruits of the harvest are brought in. He is the Firstfruits.
This is a foundation stone of our faith.

> 1 Corinthians 15:51-52 Look, I will tell you a
> secret - not all of us will die! But we will all be

changed! 52 It will take but a moment, the blink
of an eye, at the final shofar. For the shofar
will sound, and the dead will be raised to live
forever, and we too will be changed.

Yeshua is the Firstfruits of the Resurrection, that is, the
Firstfruits of those who will rise from the dead. His followers,
those "in Messiah," or as we read in I Corinthians 15:23, "those
who belong to the Messiah" are the resurrection harvest to
follow. He wants us to understand, appreciate, have faith in,
and remember His plan that those of His chosen who have
died previously and those of His chosen who are alive at that
time will one day be resurrected from the dead to be with Him
as the fullness of His resurrection harvest.

> 1 Thessalonians 4:17-*All of us who are in Him-will
> always be with the Lord.*

What does that mean? It means we'll never die again.
We'll have immortal bodies, eternal life, and we'll always be
in the glorious presence of God.

> 1 Corinthians 15:54-55 *When what decays puts
> on imperishability and what is mortal puts on
> immortality, then this passage in the Tanakh will
> be fulfilled: "Death is swallowed up in victory. 55
> "Death, where is your victory? Death, where is
> your sting?"*

So I believe that He chose to rise on Firstfruits and to
have many holy people arise that day also, so we would be
reminded of this yearly—every year—that this is His promise
to us for our future. You see, God knew we would need
periodic reminding.

This also relates to Passover because that is what
the Seder is all about. Its purpose is to help us remember
the Covenant and renew it. Again, God knows that we as
human beings are forgetful. And as I said in the Passover

book, it worked! Here it is 3500 years later and we are still remembering the Exodus and the Covenant. Firstfruits was kind of lost for hundreds of years. But thank the Lord, even without the Firstfruits Moad reminder, mostly because of the faithfulness of the church in celebrating Easter, here we are 2000 years after the Lord's Resurrection and we are still remembering that.

The event of the holy people being resurrected happened to strengthen our faith and keep in the forefront of our minds also our coming resurrection as the fullness of His resurrection harvest. This hope of our future resurrection helps to sustain us through times of trials and the difficulties of life. So let's be thankful for God's provision of Firstfruits and for those who were resurrected when Yeshua was, to remind us and encourage us.

Let's pray.

Father, we thank You for Yeshua's Resurrection. We pray that You strengthen our belief in that. That we will know for sure that if anything in the world is true, it is true that Yeshua arose from the dead. I pray that everyone reading this book would not doubt, but would have strong faith in Yeshua and His atoning sacrifice and in the power of His Resurrection.

We thank You, Father, for the holy people who were resurrected on the Day of Yeshua's Resurrection. We thank You that we will be resurrected when Yeshua returns. Make that faith strong and real in us also that we will resurrect some day.

*****

Put your hand on your chest and say, "I am going to resurrect. I will be resurrected some day. This is not the body that I'm going to spend eternity in. I'm going to have a new body, an immortal body, an eternal body."

*****

I pray, Father, that this would be a reality to us and that this hope will sustain us all of our lives. I thank You for that! In Yeshua's awesome Name. Amein!

Chapter 4

HOW THE RESURRECTION FULFILLED EXODUS AND FIRSTFRUITS

Let's just take a moment and pray.

Father, thank You for this Appointed Time, this special time. I believe You have something to say to us that is significant. So we commit this time to You. We ask You to open up our ears to hear, our eyes to see, our minds to understand, our hearts to receive, and our wills to be obedient. We just commit this to You and thank You for Your Word, and we stand against any of the forces of the enemy that would try to confuse or distract us in any way. In Yeshua's Name. Amen.

Review

So now you know that this Moad is a double Biblical holiday. It is Resurrection Day and it's Yom haBikkurim, the day of Firstfruits. As I mentioned, this day is really not kept by traditional, Rabbinic Judaism, except for the fact that it marks the beginning of the Counting of the Omer (the numbering of days) to the next holiday.

So we've already seen that significant events in the life of Yeshua all happened on Moadim. Do you remember what happened on Passover? Right! Yeshua's sacrifice on the Cross. What happened on Shavuot? Yes, the Holy Spirit came with fire!

Now to the question at hand. You know this one. What happened on the Sunday following Passover? Yes, Yeshua was resurrected! He rose from the dead. And what Biblical Moad is it according to Torah? Do you remember the Hebrew? Yes, *Yom HaBikkurim*, the Day of Firstfruits. And who pointed out the connection between Yeshua's Resurrection and Firstfruits? Yes, Rabbi Sha'ul (Paul). Do you remember the Scripture reference? Here it is again in case you forgot.

> 1 Corinthians 15:20-23 *but the fact is that the Messiah has been raised from the dead the firstfruits of those who have died. 22 For just as in connection with Adam all die, so in connection with the Messiah all will be made alive. 23 But each in his own order: the Messiah is the first-fruits; then those who belong to the Messiah, at the time of his coming;*

So now I want to do a little bit of arithmetic here about the amount of time between the Crucifixion and the Resurrection. Yeshua gave us the equation.

> Matthew 12:40 F*or just as Yonah was three days and three nights in the belly of the sea-monster, so will the Son of Man be three days and three nights in the depths of the earth.*

Some people disagree with me, but to keep in line with what Yeshua said in this verse, three days and three nights, I believe He was crucified on Thursday. Most agree that He arose on Sunday, but there are disagreements about when He died. Passover would have been the 14th of the month of

Nisan on the Jewish calendar, the lunar calendar. So to be three days later, Sunday would have been on the 17th. And then He would have been three days and three nights in the earth, fulfilling that verse.

And, of course, this disagrees with the church's traditional reckoning because, according to the church, His death was on Good Friday and then He rose on Sunday. Right? And that's three days, Friday, Saturday, Sunday, well, it is at least part of each of the three days. But Yeshua said three nights. Now, using your math skills, are you able to put three nights between Friday and Sunday? Impossible, right? Okay, you've got Friday, Friday night into Saturday night.... Nope, it doesn't work. So that's why I believe He was crucified on Thursday.

What If He Hadn't?

So, as we have seen, Yeshua fulfilled Passover and Firstfruits. Now, here's a thought. If God had not accepted the firstfruits offering of barley, the Israelites would not have had any assurance that He was going to bless the further harvest. Right? Likewise, if Yeshua hadn't risen from the dead, we would have no assurance of a resurrection harvest coming. That is, we would have no assurance that we were going to be resurrected, and it's really, really important that we have that assurance. Look at what Sha'ul says about it.

> 1 Corinthians 15:14 *And if the Messiah has not been raised, then what we have proclaimed is in vain; also your trust is in vain;*

In other words, the Gospel would be empty. It would be useless. Our faith would be in vain, useless, empty!

> 1 Corinthians 15:16-17 *For if the dead are not raised, then the Messiah has not been raised either; 17 and if the Messiah has not been raised, your trust is useless, and you are still in your sins.*

He's pretty adamant about this that the Resurrection is pretty important. There would be no evidence for the atonement, no forgiveness of sins, no possibility of a relationship with God.

> 1 Corinthians 15:18 *Also, if this is the case, those who died in union with the Messiah are lost.*

Believers would be lost! I've struggled with this verse a little. I mean He still would have died, sacrificing His life and His Blood to pay the price for our sins, wouldn't He? But here's the thing. Believers would be lost because there would be no living Messiah, no Messiah for us to follow. There would be no possibility of a relationship with God. Why? Because you can't have a personal living relationship with a dead person. Right?

> 1 Corinthians 15:20 *but the fact is that Messiah has been raised from the dead, the Firstfruits of those who would have died.*

Hallelujah! That's something we do need to praise the Lord for! So now you see how important that is!

I've done a lot of funerals, and let me tell you that there is a real difference between a funeral where people don't believe they're ever going to see the person again and a funeral where people have this hope of the resurrection. What an enormous difference it is! A tremendous difference! So having this hope of resurrection is very important.

While It Was Still Dark

So now I'd like to go in another direction. There's another amazing connection between Firstfruits and the Resurrection. This is a connection that exposes what we call a Jewish Root. This is like if you were standing by a tree and you were looking down where the roots are, think of the big roots right at the bottom of the trunk that stick up out of the ground. This is one of those big fat roots. It's a really big root that's there. It's amazing what this root is.

So let's look, first of all, at two questions. When exactly did Yeshua rise from the dead? And do we know for sure it was on a Sunday?

> John 20:1 *Early on the first day of the week, while it was still dark, Miryam from Magdala (Mary Magdalene) went to the tomb and saw that the stone had been removed from the tomb.*

Notice that it was still dark, but she could see that the stone had been removed. So what did she do? She went to get Peter and John and that would have taken her some time. And John got there first.

> John 20:5-7 *Stooping down, he saw the linen burial-sheets lying there but did not go in. 6 Then, following him, Shim`on Kefa (Simon Peter) ar- rived, entered the tomb and saw the burial-sheets lying there, 7 also the cloth that had been around his head, lying not with the sheets but in a sep- arate place and still folded up. 8 Then the other talmid (disciple), who had arrived at the tomb first, also went in; he saw, and he trusted.*

Now what's missing here is no mention of a light. Notice that there's no mention that they needed a candle or they needed to light a fire or they, you know, needed to take up their smartphones. *smile* So the sun has come up by this time.

Now I've been to Israel. Have you been to Israel? They have what some people believe actually is the tomb, but at least is an example of what the tomb was like. It is not a structure like we have in our cemeteries. It's a cave in a cliff and the stone is rolled away. If you try to go in there, it's dark.

It's dark in there! So that morning sun, low in the east must have been shining right into the tomb for them to be able to see all that.

> John 20:11 *but Miryam (Mary) stood outside crying. As she cried, she bent down, peered into the tomb,*

So what we see here is that she stood outside crying the whole time while Peter and John were looking in and then going in.

> John 20:11b-12a *...she ... peered into the tomb, 12 and saw two angels in white sitting where the body of Yeshua had been, one at the head and one at the feet.*

Now here's something amazing. Think a minute about where those angels are positioned. It doesn't say this, but what if they were facing each other? Does that make you think of anything? Something in the Torah about the Temple? Maybe you got it now. Think of the Aron Brit, the Ark of the Covenant! It had two angels facing each other over the *Kapporet*, the Mercy Seat. (*Kapporet* means place of atonement. It comes from the same root word that kippur comes from, kippur means atonement.) What if those angels had wings that were reaching over where Yeshua's body was and were touching? Doesn't that just give you revelation chills? Two angels were there on each side of where His body had been, which was the sacrifice of mercy, atoning for our sins. Whoa! Astounding! He is the fulfillment the Ark of the Covenant and the Mercy Seat!! Praise His Name.

Now, getting back to Miryam (Mary), when she saw those angels, what would've been the first thing she would have done? She would have called Peter and John back, if they had still been around. Right? So she must have stood outside crying long enough that they had gotten so far away that she couldn't call them back. The angels spoke to her.

> John 20:13-14 *"Why are you crying?" they asked her.*
> *"They took my Lord," she said to them, "and I don't know where they have put him." 14 As she said this, she turned around and saw Yeshua standing there, but she didn't know it was he.*

This was the first time Yeshua was seen resurrected.

> John 20:15-16 *Yeshua said to her, "Lady, why are you crying? Whom are you looking for?"*
> *Thinking he was the gardener, she said to him, "Sir, if you're the one who carried him away, just tell me where you put him; and I'll go and get him myself." 16*
> *Yeshua said to her, "Miryam!"*
> *Turning, she cried out to him in Hebrew, "Rabbani!" (that is, "Teacher!")*

Evidently when He said her name, it was said in such a way that she recognized that this was the One she loved. So it's great to recall this part of the Resurrection event, but what I want to emphasize here, from back in verse 1, is that it was still dark when she saw that the stone was rolled away. Then she went somewhere to get Peter and John. They came back. We don't know how far that was. The sun must have been up enough to see inside the tomb, and Mary stood outside crying.

So what we see here is, it was three days after Passover right around dawn. It wasn't like in the middle of the night. It was right around dawn because the sun came up during that time. Do you see that? I know I went through a long thing to show that, but it's important to see it.

So that was the first time it was seen that Yeshua was

resurrected, and it was right around dawn on that early Sunday morning. Okay?

Symbolic Death and Resurrection

Now to the Jewish root. Going back to the Israelites coming out of Egypt, Rabbi Sha'ul wrote some very interesting things about it.

> I Corinthians 10:1 *For, brothers, I don't want you to miss the significance of what happened to our fathers. All of them were guided by the pillar of cloud, and they all passed through the sea,*

So obviously he's referring here to the dividing of the Red Sea for the Israelites to pass through when they escaped from Egypt.

> I Corinthians 10:2 *and in connection with the cloud and with the sea they all immersed themselves into Moshe (Moses),*

So what does this mean? Well, Rabbi Sha'ul understood that the passing of the Israelites through the waters of the Red Sea led by the cloud of God was an immersion or a baptism into Moses. In other words, it was symbolic of marking Israel's entry into the Mosaic or Sinai Covenant, just as immersion in Yeshua's Name is a person's ceremony of bringing them into the New Covenant. You see the parallel there? The Israelites went through the waters and when they came out they were Covenant people. When a person comes to believe in Yeshua, they go into the water, and they come out as what? A covenant person. It's the ceremony of entrance into God's family. And Rabbi Sha'ul understood a deeper meaning of immersion.

> Romans 6:4a *Through immersion into his death...*

This is speaking of being immersed into the Messiah.

> Romans 6:4b ...*we were buried with him; so that just as, through the glory of the Father, the Messiah was raised from the dead, likewise we too might live a new life.*

So in what we call *t'vilah* in Hebrew, immersion in English, going under the water is symbolic of the death of the old person. For us, you know, sometimes you could think that now that scuba gear has been invented, people can survive underwater, but in those days, there was no scuba gear. So if you were underwater for more than about a minute and a half, that was it, you were dead.

So then coming up out of the water to new life in the Messiah is symbolic of resurrecting as a new creation, born again from above, all things new. So according to Romans 6 verse 4 (above), Rabbi Sha'ul is understanding immersion in this way, that it's a death and a resurrection.

But then if we go back to what he was saying in 1 Corinthians 10, we see that he understood the passing of the Israelites under a cloud through the Red Sea as an immersion and a death and a resurrection: from death and slavery in Egypt to new life and freedom in the Promised Land. Do you see that? I know it's a stretch to grasp these things. So we have this understanding from Sha'ul. This is what he's writing about in 1 Corinthians 10, that the Israelites going through the Red Sea could be seen as an immersion, going down into the waters of death and coming up to new life in the Kingdom of God.

The Huge Jewish Root

But when exactly did that resurrection of the Israelites occur? What day of the month?

Exodus 12:6 (This is speaking of the lamb.)
You are to keep it until the fourteenth day of the
month, and then the entire assembly of the com-
munity of Isra'el will slaughter it at dusk.

So that's when Passover is. The Passover lamb was slaughtered at sundown on the 14th of Nisan or Aviv, the first month of the year in the Biblical calendar.

Exodus 12:6-8 *You must watch over it until the*
fourteenth day of the same month. Then the
whole assembly of the congregation of Israel is
to slaughter it at twilight. 7 They are to take the
blood and put it on the two doorposts and on the
crossbeam of the houses where they will eat it. 8
They are to eat the meat that night, roasted over a
fire. With matzot and bitter herbs they are to eat it.

Exodus 12:18 *During the first month in the eve-*
ning of the fourteenth day of the month, you are
to eat matzot, until the evening of the twenty-first
day of the month.

Then that night, because remember in the Jewish calendar the days begin at sundown, so that night they left Egypt in the middle of the night. That's the first day of unleavened bread or the first day of Passover. They left in the middle of the night. That would have been the night of the 14th. So that was sundown on the 14th, into the night of still the 14th. Then in Exodus 12:37, we read that they camped at a place called Sukkot after the first day. That would have been the night of the 15th, sundown on the 15th. And then it gets a little tricky.

Exodus 12:37 T*hen Bnei-Yisrael journeyed from*
Rameses to Succoth, about 600,000 men on foot,
as well as children.

Next they camped at Etham.

Exodus 13:20 *So they journeyed from Succoth*
and encamped in Etham, on the edge of the
wilderness.

That would have been sunset on the 16th and all night that night. Then it says God told them to turn around and camp at Pi Hahiroth.

> Exodus 14:2 *"Speak to Bnei-Yisrael, so that they turn back and encamp before Pi-hahiroth, between Migdol and the sea. You are to camp by the sea,"*

So now we are at sunset on the 17th. So we have them at the shore of the Red Sea on the evening of the 17th when they were trapped by Pharaoh's army.

So, all night on day 17, they have the pillar of fire and the "angel of God" and darkness behind them, protecting them from Pharoh's army (Exodus 14:19-20). At the same time, Moses has held up his rod and a wind is blowing the Red Sea all night (verse 21.).

Then it says, on the morning of the 17th, three days after leaving Egypt on Passover, God divided the Red Sea, and they went through and the Egyptian army which followed them was destroyed. So in fulfillment of the promise God made to Moses before he went to Pharaoh, two things happened here.

The promise is in Exodus 6:6-7. We always go over this during our Passover Seder. One of the phrases in Exodus 6:6 is *I will redeem you with an outstretched arm and with great judgments.* So the Israelites were redeemed. Their slave masters no longer owned them. God took possession of them. They had belonged to God when they went down to Egypt, but then they became owned by somebody else. So now they were redeemed. That's what redeeming means. When you bring your bottle back to the redemption center at the supermarket, the supermarket buys back what they owned before which you bought from them for a nickel.

So the Israelites were redeemed. How? With the judgments, and the destruction of the Egyptian army when Pharaoh went to bring them back.

So this is remembered by one of the cups of the Passover Seder. Right? The Cup of Redemption. But then in verse 7 it says this *I will take you to myself as a people and I will be your God.* So when the people were redeemed after they came up out of the water, they were now a people who belonged to God. And this is remembered in the Seder with the Cup of the Kingdom. So the immersion in water of the Israelites escaping Egypt was symbolic of their death—the death of the people who were slaves of the Egyptians—and the coming up from the water was symbolic of their resurrection—the resurrection as a people who were God's people. Did you follow all of that?

Same Moad, Same Time, Same day

Okay, when does this resurrection happen? Well, we know it was on the 17th, three days after Passover, but the Bible even tells us the time of day!

> Exodus 14:27 *So Moses stretched his hand out over the waters, and the sea returned to its strength at the break of dawn. The Egyptians were fleeing from it, but ADONAI overthrew them in the midst of the sea.*

So the symbolic resurrection when the sea returned was at the break of dawn, three days after Passover—on Firstfruits! And thus the Israelites' passage in the Red Sea and the destruction of the Egyptian army fulfilled Firstfruits. They were the firstfruits of those who became part of God's Kingdom. Isn't that incredible?!

Now what did we find out about the timing of Yeshua's death and resurrection? When was Yeshua resurrected?

Three days after Passover. What time of day? At the break of dawn! The same day, same time, same Moad, same Appointed Time of Firstfruits. So the Resurrection of Yeshua fulfilled not only the Firstfruits like Paul talks about, His being the Firstfruits of those who rise from the dead, but Yeshua's resurrection also fulfilled the symbolic resurrection of the Israelites when they passed through the Red Sea, and it was on the same day and the exact same time of day!

Here's the timeline list:

- Left Egypt on 1st day of Unleavened Bread in the middle of the night of the 14th of Nissan.
- Exodus 12:32 camped at Sukkot at sunset on the 15th
- Exodus 13:20 camped at Etam at sunset on the 16th
- But Exodus 14:2 says God turned them around
- Camped at Pi-Hachirot at sunset on 17th at the shore of the Red Sea, trapped by Pharaoh's army
- God divided the Red Sea & they went through it at dawn on the Day of Firstfruits, still on the 17th, three days & three nights after the lambs were slaughtered

Another Fulfilling

Now here's another side to this concerning the destruction of the Egyptian army. When the waters returned, they were destroyed. They were the ones who would have gone and taken the Israelites back into captivity, back into slavery. That's what they came out for. "Oh our slaves got away! Let's go get them and bring them back!" Right? That was also fulfilled by Yeshua when He rose from the dead. He explained it to John.

> Revelation 4:17-18 *I am the First and the Last, 18 the Living One. [I resurrected!] I was dead, but look! — I am alive forever and ever! And I hold the keys to Death and Sh'ol.*

Death and hell were defeated by Yeshua's Resurrection, just as the Egyptian army was defeated when the Israelites came out of the Red Sea. So just as the Israelites were symbolically immersed in the waters of the Red Sea, every believer, who is immersed, is symbolically participating not only in Yeshua's death and resurrection but in Israel's death and resurrection in the Book of Exodus. The waters of the Red Sea and the waters of immersion were designed by God to be like a parallel experience. In immersion in the death and Resurrection of Yeshua, every believer experiences personal liberation from where? The Haggadah says from Egypt because Egypt represents this world. And now we know that the Resurrection of Yeshua and of Israel happened at the exact same time, at dawn on this same day, Firstfruits. Amazing! Let's give God praise! The timing is just so amazing!

Hallelujah!! Thank You, Father! You are so awesome! You are glorious! You design everything so marvelously! Praise Your Name!

God is outside of time, but He can move things around in time, so they happen completely synchronized, so that it just makes everything connect, and you can see all these things. Praise His Name!!

(Now I'm wondering. Do you suppose we Messianics will ever celebrate Firstfruits in the future at the break of dawn in remembrance of this exact, synchronized timing? It was just a thought. We'll see.)

Firstfruit Offering Today

In our praise and adoration of Elohim, after seeing how He worked the timing out so astoundingly, it makes us want to do all we can to bless Him and honor Him and glorify Him, including giving offerings to Him. Right? So, amazingly, as we learned earlier, there is an offering commanded for Resurrection/Firstfruits Day. Let's look at that offering.

So in Biblical times, Bikkurim/Firstfruits was a day of celebration, of giving thanks for the crops being harvested, and also for celebrating with a Firstfruits offering. If you're not that familiar with agriculture, in an agricultural society there are many harvests, one for each type of crop. Like in the spring in my home area, we come to one of my favorite harvests, the strawberry harvest. Then later, it will be the corn harvest, and after that the tomato harvest. So there's lots of harvests. As we learned earlier, the Firstfruit offering was made in faith that in giving the first of the barley to the Lord, to be sacrificed to Him, God would bless the rest of the harvest through the rest of the year. The wheat harvest that comes later is the bigger harvest, and that's on Shavuot. So that's also a harvest festival, where you give another firstfruit offering.

So how does this apply to us today? Well, we traditionally end our service on Bikkurim/Firstfruits/Resurrection Day by coming up front in a processional, as in Biblical days, and giving our firstfruits offerings. Now understand there's no compulsion as to the amount. This is a freewill offering. It's not like the tithe. It's an amount not specified in the Bible. Well, it does say an omer of barley, but we are not giving barley, and an omer doesn't quite transfer to finances.

Here's how I figure it, but this is just me. You can figure it your own way. The Biblical year starts on the first day of this month, Nissan. Firstfruits is on the 17th day of Nissan. So by then, we have worked for two weeks into the Biblical year. So that's kind of how I think about it. I do a tithe on my firstfruits. I've already tithed on it, but this is like an offering from those firstfruits. So like I said that's just an example. There's no compulsion. This is totally up to each person what's in your heart.

Five Kinds of Kingdom Fruits

But I want to point out something else. The Bible tells us there are other kinds of the fruits. Okay? You and I produce fruits that trees don't produce. Here's an example

> Galatians 5:22-23a *But the fruit of the Spirit is love, joy, peace, patience, kindness, goodness, faithfulness, 23 humility, self control.*

So the fruit of the Spirit is Godly character, and it's not visible. Its internal. So that's one of the kind of fruits. There are actually five different kinds of fruits that we produce.

The second is from Hebrews 12:11 when speaking about God's discipline in us.

> Hebrews 12:11b ... *for those who have been trained by it (by God's discipline), it later produces its peaceful fruit, which is righteousness.*

So we also produce the fruit of righteousness, which I kind of loosely define as living in victory over sin and taking Godly stands—on issues, on morality, on compassion, on justice—in places where we need to stand up and say, "No, that's not right. This is what the Bible says." So that's the fruit of righteousness.

The third is the fruit of our lips, praising God continually—not just praising God when we come to service and singing some songs, but continually praising God in all our speech, having a God-praising attitude, an attitude of gratitude about life, and just being thankful. So that's the third fruit, the fruit of our lips.

The fourth fruit is the fruit of our good works. What are our good works? Helping the needy, helping our friends, organizing other people to help, teaching the Word, giving to the Kingdom—and not just doing them. In Matthew 5:16, Yeshua tells us to let our light shine. So doing good works, but also letting people know that these are inspired by the God of the Bible. That's letting our light shine. So that's the fourth fruit.

The fifth fruit is very interesting. Our offspring are called our fruit. So our physical children are our fruit, but also our spiritual children, those whom we disciple, those whom we have an input into their lives are our spiritual children.

So have you had any fruits in your life so far? In the last few weeks, has the Holy Spirit born the fruit of good character in your life? Often that comes through trials. Have you borne the fruit of righteousness, taking a stand against something ungodly? Or have you had some victory over sin? Have you borne the fruit of praise, giving God the glory, having a thankful attitude? Have you borne the fruit of good works, simply helping someone else? Have you borne the fruit of physical or spiritual children, even speaking a word to someone that bore fruit in their life?

So, if so, today you can give a thank offering for these spiritual fruits to the Lord, as well as an offering of the firstfruits of your labor.

Let's Pray

So Father, we thank You for this opportunity to bring our firstfruits before You, and we do it in faith, believing that You are going to bless the rest of the harvests. So we pray, Father, for each of our lives, that there will be a harvest of the fruits of the Spirit, that we would have love and joy and peace and patience and kindness and gentleness and self-control. And we pray, Father, there would be a harvest of praise, that we would have attitudes of thanksgiving, that we would be thankful. We pray, Lord, that there would be a harvest of righteousness, that we would have victory over sin, that we would be bold and take stands against unrighteousness.

We pray that there would be a harvest of good works, that we would be able to let our light shine by being able to help people, and give You glory through that. And finally, Lord, even as our children represent the fruit of parenting, we pray, Father, for our children to be blessed and to be led by Your Spirit, to know You. We also pray, Father, for our spiritual children, for those whom we teach, those whom we witness to, those whom we disciple, those whom we help, that they would be blessed and grow in their walk with You. And we pray that we would see a great increase in the number of spiritual children. In Yeshua's mighty, all-powerful Name. Amen.

Chapter 5
OPENING THE EYES

Dayenu! But There's More!

> I Corinthians 5:7 ... *For our Pesach lamb, the Messiah, has been sacrificed.*

Rabbi Sha'ul calls Yeshua the Firstfruits, as we have seen, and our Passover Lamb. So the Messiah who died on Pesakh and who arose on Firstfruits is the Passover Lamb and the Firstfruit. If you have firstfruits, it means you have to have second, third, and later fruits. Right? And hallelujah, our resurrection will be part of that later fruit!

Now let me lay it out again, this whole earth-shaking week between Pesakh and Firstfruits, so we can really grasp it. The way we understand the timing, to make it correct—three days and three nights—it was on Wednesday evening that He had the Last Seder (also called the Last Supper).

Then that night was when He spent the night in the Garden of Gethsemane. It was the Garden vigil. (See my book on Pesakh to find out what that means.) And it was later that night toward Thursday morning that He was betrayed and arrested, and then was falsely accused by those who were envious of His anointing.

Later on Thursday morning He was tried, beaten, whipped, and forced to carry His own Cross. Thursday afternoon He was crucified and died at the same time the Passover lambs were being slaughtered. So He was in the grave, Thursday night, Friday night, and Saturday night.

We understand all this now because we understand that there were two Seders. There was one Wednesday night and then another one on Thursday night on the 14th of Nissan. (Again, see my Pesakh, Passover book to learn how we know this and why there were two.)

We have looked at what I think is really mysterious and awesome, that after He died and His body was put into the tomb, His spirit went into Heaven. According to Hebrews 9, He went into the Holy of Holies in the Heavenly Temple, and offered His Blood as the atoning sacrifice on Heaven's Mercy Seat.

Then we saw in Scripture that He went into hell and proclaimed victory over the forces of Satan, and He took the key of Hell, and it says that He triumphed over death. So He took the key of death also. Then, sometime after His Resurrection, He led the Saints out from Abraham's bosom where they had been waiting safely, the Godly people from the Tanakh, Old Testament, like Moses and Daniel, etc., and He led them, along with the ones who were seen alive, into the presence of God.

So what I have to say to that is something out of the Passover Seder which you can say with me. DAYENU! DAYENU! It would have been enough!! Right?!

But there's more! And the more is that He's alive! And because He's alive we can have a living relationship with Him. You know, if He wasn't alive, for us to say we have a relationship with Him, that we're hearing from Him, and we're talking to Him, that would be like people who are trying to communicate with the dead. And it is forbidden in the Torah. But hallelujah, He really is alive! Hallelujah!!

Mysterious Resurrected Body

So now I just thought we would look through a passage about what happened on Resurrection day 2000 years ago that we don't often look at or go into much depth on. It's a story that happened on the day that He arose. It starts out with two of Yeshua's talmidim (disciples) on the road to *Amma'us,* Emmaus. We know the name of one. His name is Cleopis, but we don't know the name of the other, so I will just call him his friend.

> Luke 24:13-16 *That same day, two of them were going toward a village about seven miles from Yerushalayim called Amma'us, 14 and they were talking with each other about all the things that had happened. 15 As they talked and discussed, Yeshua himself came up and walked along with them, 16 but something kept them from recognizing him.*

So right away here we see this thing about Him being alive that is really amazing because He just kind of showed up and is walking along with them. And also we see here kind of confirmation of what happened with Miriam (Mary Magdalene). Remember when she saw Him when He first appeared, she didn't recognized Him. They're not recognizing Him either.

So there must be something different about His resurrected body. We know that eventually they did recognize Him. I saw something in this that I think the Lord wants us to apply to ourselves. I think the Lord does this for us every once in a while. He comes up alongside us and walks with us and we don't realize He's there. But He is there! So keep that in mind.

> Luke 24:17 *He asked them, "What are you talking about with each other as you walk along?" They stopped short, their faces downcast;*

Now also understand that His voice must've been different, too, because they didn't recognize Him by His voice either. And you know Miriam (Mary) recognized Him when He called her name. I think what happened there was He spoke her name in a way that she was familiar with—in a way that maybe nobody else spoke to her, and so that's why she recognized Him. But these two didn't recognize his voice.

They begin to tell Yeshua all the events that had just happened to Him. Of course, He didn't need to be told. He knew all this, but that's what they had been talking about: all the events of His crucifixion and the disappearance of His body. Now, what was really significant as I read through those verses, which I'm summarizing here, is that when they talked about Him to Him, they called Him a prophet. I thought, "That's kind of interesting. They didn't call Him the Messiah." There's a lot of Jewish people today who think He is a prophet, but they don't think He is the Messiah. So it's interesting to see where they're thinking was.

> Luke 24:25 *He said to them, "Foolish people! So unwilling to put your trust in everything the prophets spoke! 26 Didn't the Messiah have to die like this before entering his glory?" 27 Then, starting with Moshe and all the prophets, he explained to them the things that can be found throughout the Tanakh concerning himself.*

And I just thought of a couple of things He might have been telling them, like, for example, about Him having to die.

> Isaiah 53:8.(CJB) *After forcible arrest and sen-*
> *tencing, he was taken away; and none of his*
> *generation protested his being cut off from the*
> *land of the living for the crimes of my people,*
> *who deserved the punishment themselves.*

Being "cut off from the land of the living" is being killed.

> Isaiah 53:10 *Yet it pleased ADONAI to bruise*
> *Him. He caused Him to suffer. If He makes*
> *His soul a guilt offering, He will see His off-*
> *spring, He will prolong His days, and the will of*
> *ADONAI will succeed by His hand.*

I don't know about you, but that's speaking to me. He got "cut off from the land of the living," but what else happened? "He will prolong His days"—He was resurrected! So He's telling His disciples about all this and then because it was getting dark, they stopped at an inn for a meal.

> Luke 24:30 *As he was reclining with them at the*
> *table, he took the matzah, made the b'rakhah,*
> *broke it and handed it to them. 31 Then their*
> *eyes were opened, and they recognized him.*
> *But he became invisible to them. [WOW!] 32*
> *They said to each other, "Didn't our hearts burn*
> *inside us as he spoke to us on the road, open-*
> *ing up the Tanakh to us?"*

Meetings with Resurrected Messiah

Then Cleopis and his friend returned to Jerusalem and the other eleven where they reported what had happened, and they heard reports from the eleven about Yeshua rising from the dead. And while they were all talking, probably very excitedly, about all this, Yeshua appeared in the midst of all of them. He told them not to doubt. This

time He allowed them to touch Him, and He ate some fish
with them.

> Luke 24:44-49 *Yeshua said to them, "This is*
> *what I meant when I was still with you and*
> *told you that everything written about me in*
> *the Torah of Moshe, the Prophets and the*
> *Psalms had to be fulfilled." 45 Then he opened*
> *their minds, so that they could understand the*
> *Tanakh, 46 telling them, "Here is what it says:*
> *the Messiah is to suffer and to rise from the*
> *dead on the third day; 47 and in his name re-*
> *pentance leading to forgiveness of sins is to be*
> *proclaimed to people from all nations, starting*
> *with Yerushalayim."*

So, here He commissioned them to spread the Good
News of His resurrection and of salvation to those who put
their trust in Him. Notice also. It's very important to see
this. You know how we think about the Word of the Lord
coming to Peter and sending him to the Gentiles in Acts
10? But when Yeshua gave the Great Commission, He
sent them to the nations, the Gentiles! They just didn't go
until the tenth chapter of Acts when the Lord had to give
Peter that vision.

> Luke 24:48-49 *"You are witnesses of these*
> *things. 49 Now I am sending forth upon you*
> *what my Father promised, so stay here in the*
> *city until you have been equipped with power*
> *from above."*

Now He is saying to wait for the power of the Holy
Spirit on Shavuot. Although it's pretty obvious, and we
have looked at how John describes this, that they had
received the Holy Spirit at this point, but not the power.
And some of the evidence that they had received the Holy

Spirit is that now they can understand the Scriptures. But the power wasn't there until 50 days later.

Then He departed to Heaven and they were full of joy. So that's how the day ended on that first Resurrection day.

In Acts chapter 1, Luke records their meetings with Yeshua continuing for forty days. They met with Him and they talked with Him. And then Luke tells about Yeshua's final departure into Heaven when two angels say that He's going to come back the way they saw Him go.

Mark records this meeting much like Luke does. However, I think it is another meeting that Matthew records. He describes a meeting with Yeshua and His disciples on a hill in Galilee rather than in Jerusalem.

John records the same event but with some very important details. One of them is where Yeshua breathes on them and says, "Receive the Holy Spirit." The other is where Yeshua tells them that they have the power to forgive sin in their hands. So all of the Gospels confer that these meetings happened, but are just a little bit different on the details. (See the chart in Appendix A of this book to compare them all.)

Hearts Burning

So as I read this over, there were four details in Luke's account that just really jumped out at me. I prayed and the Lord showed me some things about this that I want to share with you. One of the details is a burning in verse 32 where they were reporting on this and they said, "Didn't our hearts burn inside us?" And the other three are openings. Verse 31 says that their eyes were opened and they recognized Him. In verse 32, He opened up the Tanakh or the Scriptures to them. And in verse 45, He opened their minds so they could understand the Tanakh.

So as I read those, I was asking the Lord, why these different phrases? What do these phrases mean? As I prayed about this, I began to see some things here.

When Cleopis and his friend described their experienced when Yeshua spoke to them on the road, they mentioned the burning, "Didn't our hearts burn inside us?" [My first thought was kind of silly. Did He give them heartburn? Just kidding. I don't think He gave them heartburn!] In the Scriptures, the heart often is a synonym for the spirit—the spirit of man. And in the Amplified Bible, it says it this way

> Luke 24:32 (AMP) *"Was not our heart greatly moved and burning within us...?"*

So what does this mean when our hearts burn or are moved? The way I understand this is they were having a spiritual experience. And we know that according to the "law of kinds," spirits speak to spirits. So what was happening here was that the Holy Spirit was speaking to the spirits of these two men. He was speaking through Yeshua to them even though they didn't realize it was Yeshua yet.

This imagery here of the Holy Spirit burning is also very significant, because in other places the Holy Spirit is described as fire. There was fire on the heads of the disciples on Shavuot in Acts. In Exodus there was a pillar of fire and a burning bush. So the Spirit was coming as fire.

So here's what I think was happening. They were describing that the fire of the Holy Spirit was lighting their spirits on fire, even though they probably didn't realize it was the Holy Spirit. Somehow, while they walked along as Yeshua was explaining Scriptures to them, there was like an awakening.

You've got to put yourself in the place of these two disciples. These guys were really down! This was three days after He had been killed! And they had all these expectations of Him of what He was going to do, and how their lives were going to change and how all of Israel was going to change, but now He was dead! And now there were these rumors coming up. "Oh, somebody saw Him alive." You can see that they might have been in kind of a distressed state. "Do we believe the rumor? Do we not believe it?"

But what was happening was Yeshua was walking along side them and He was bringing their spirits to life. He was telling them that this was supposed to happen. He was showing them and helping them understand that all of this was foretold in the Scriptures.

So how does this apply to us? I think this applies to me because I think I've had it happen to me. I think you probably recognize that sometimes it happens to you, I hope it does, that the Spirit of God causes your spirit to become passionate about something, become concerned about something, become alive about something. Maybe you see some injustice, or you see a great need or a great opportunity. You don't necessarily have a word from the Lord, but all of a sudden it's like this is really important. I've got to do something about this.

Have you ever had an experience like that? I believe it is the Spirit of God working and awakening your spirit. What I saw in this is that we need to learn to be aware of these fires. We need to be able to recognize them, so that we know when the Lord is directing us in a certain direction.

Opening Our Understanding

Then we have the three openings. The first opening was on the road.

Luke 24:32 *"opening up the Tanakh to us."*

This happened before they recognized Him. He opened the Scripture to them before they recognized Him. Now, of course, we understand that the only Scripture they had was the Tanakh, the Old Testament at this time. And He began to reveal how He had to fulfill the prophecies and that He had to die, and why He had to die and rise from the dead. To me, what this meant is that when He opened the Tanakh to them, it became comprehensible to them, and they began to understand it.

This brought me back to my own spiritual journey. I remember it was before I became a believer that the Scriptures began to be opened to me. When I was still just a seeker, I began to understand the Scriptures. They began to be important to me. I was just seeking at that time. It was dramatically different because before I had become a seeker, the Scriptures were closed to me. In fact, I took a class in college. It was called Literature from the Bible. I remember I had to read parts of it, probably mostly from Old Testament literary writings, such as the Psalms and prophets, etc. I had to study them, and write papers on those parts. But it had no meaning for me. It was totally empty, totally meaningless. It was just not my time. I was not ready for it.

But when I became a seeker, it was different. I went to my wife Diane and said, "I think I want to read the Bible because you're reading the Bible so much." I wanted to read the Bible, and because I was a seeker—seeking God for truth, He began to reveal it to me. I remember as I read the book of John, which was the first book I read, it was like John had a hold of me by my shirt and was shaking me. The words were shaking me and I wanted to be a follower of the Messiah. I wasn't a believer yet, but I wanted to be a follower of Him.

What came to my mind was John 14:26 where Yeshua tells us this:

> John 14:26 *But the Counselor, the Ruach HaKodesh, whom the Father will send in my name, will teach you everything; that is, he will remind you of everything I have said to you.*

So it's the Holy Spirit that does that in us, that makes the Scripture come alive to a person. And what is important to understand here is that the Holy Spirit was upon me before I was a believer. Do you see that? I hadn't received Him yet, but the Spirit was revealing these things to me before I even recognized who Yeshua was. It was because I was looking for Him. I was seeking His help. I was on a quest, longing for Him.

The reason this is important is because all of us have loved ones or acquaintances that we have shared with, and we haven't seen any reaction to it yet. But what we have to understand is that once you begin to share the Scriptures with people—that's a seed—and the Holy Spirit will take what you have said and will begin bringing it alive in them before they become believers. So I like to pray for people that the Spirit of God would begin to speak to them, would begin to reveal truth to them, would begin to give them a desire to read the Word. And when they do read the Word, like happened to me, that the Word would begin to shake them.

I remember that I was very ignorant of the Gospel story. It might be hard for some to realize this, but as a Jewish young man, I didn't know how the story would end. Can you grasp what that would've been like reading through a Gospel? I didn't know how it would end! So, I was on the edge of my seat reading because I didn't know what was going to happen to Yeshua. I know it is hard to imagine anyone not knowing that, but that's how ignorant I was about it. And it just shook me when He was executed and then getting to His rising from dead, it was just awesome!

So I believe the Spirit of God is saying that this continues to happen after salvation as we continue to walk with the Lord. The Spirit of God will open passages of Scripture to us, and we'll understand something that we didn't understand before. Just for example, if you read through that passage in Leviticus about Firstfruits and Shavuot, it ends by saying to leave the grain in the field for the widows and the orphans. I remember when I first put that together, and I was thinking, "Wow this really shows how much God cares for widows and orphans. It was like a little insight. God really cares! It was like a new revelation of the character of God that I was seeing there. That's an example of the Scriptures being opened up to us.

So the first opening was that He opened the Scriptures to them.

Opening Our Eyes to Recognize

The second opening happened when Yeshua broke matzah with them,

> Luke 24:31 *said the blessing and their eyes were open and they recognized Him.*

This is a supernatural work of the Holy Spirit in their lives. I believe what's happening here is what I like to call opening their spiritual eyes. We all have spiritual eyes and ears. We have physical eyes and ears, but this was opening their spiritual eyes. Their physical eyes were open. They had seen Him for quite awhile. They talked about Him as a prophet, but until their spiritual eyes were opened, they didn't recognize Him as the Messiah.

And today in this world there are millions of people who see pictures of Yeshua through art and movies and video. Or they hear descriptions about Him from sermons or they read books. They see Him with their physical eyes or hear about Him with their physical ears, but they don't recognize who He is. They don't even understand what His title means. They might have heard His Name, Jesus Christ, but they don't understand that "Christ" means "the Anointed One," the Messiah. Or they might have heard the word "Messiah," but they don't have a clue—millions of people have no clue—what that means. They're seeing with their physical eyes and hearing with their physical ears, but they don't recognize who He is.

And here's what's really important. They don't recognize how important He is to their personal lives. He is irrelevant to them. He is just another famous character out of history, or a great author or teacher. I know because I spent many years with closed spiritual eyes and ears.

For these two men, the opening happened when they understood that this was their Messiah. This was the man who had been walking with them for three years, and now they recognized that He was their Messiah, their Lord.

It's kind of easy to understand why my eyes were so closed because of my history. Because my parents were so against religion, that reading of the Bible in college was all the reading I had ever done, except when I studied for my Bar Mitzvah. It's also easy to understand when the Good News goes to people all around world where they've never had the Scriptures, why they would not be able to see, why they would not be able to understand. But Rabbi Sha'ul predicted that the same thing would happen even to Jewish people who know the Scriptures well.

II Corinthians 3:14 *What is more, their minds were made stonelike; for to this day the same veil remains over them when they read the Old Covenant; it has not been unveiled, because only by the Messiah is the veil taken away.*

So the veil over my heart kept me from recognizing Yeshua as the Messiah for a long, long time. And that same veil is over the hearts of Jewish people who don't believe. The next verse tells us how the veil can be removed.

II Corinthians 3:16 *"But," says the Torah, "whenever someone turns to ADONAI, the veil is taken away."*

So what does that mean, "whenever someone turns to ADONAI"? When we turn to Him as a source of help in our time of need, that's how I see it. When I turned to the Lord for help, the veil over my heart was removed. See, in my case, I had turned to many other gods. What I was really looking for was meaning in my life, and I turned to the gods of other religions and different pursuits and studies and things like that.

When I decided to read the Bible, it was like I was saying, "I want to see what Yeshua has to offer to give me meaning in life." And so I turned to Him. Nothing or nobody else had given me meaning. And when I did turn to Him, the Messiah removed that veil and I recognized Him. I recognized Him first of all as an important historical figure who I knew nothing about, which made me feel quite stupid. Then I realized that He was the person I wanted to follow.

The Holy Spirit has shown me something about this veil over Jewish eyes. You know if you weave a piece of cloth, there are threads that go vertical and threads that go horizontal. Well, I believe there are two sets of threads that make up the veil. The first thread is Christian anti-Semitism, the history of conflict between the church and the Jewish people, centuries of persecution of our people in "Christian" nations. That causes Jewish people to believe that since the guidebook of all those people who persecuted us is the New Testament, it must be a book about anti-Semitism. What else could it be? That's actually what I thought. That was one of things that kept me from reading it. That was the veil. That is one set of threads.

The other set of threads is a false teaching by both the church and Jewish non-Messianic rabbis that you can't be Jewish and be a follower of Yeshua; that once you follow Him, you are not Jewish anymore, and you have to forsake everything Jewish. But it's wrong! That's why our congregation exists—to combat this false belief! That second set of threads is a huge reason for our existence. We are here as a Messianic congregation as a public witness to the Jewish community around us that you can be Jewish and be a follower of the Messiah. We hope to help unravel that particular thread in the veil.

I also recognize that the opening of my spiritual eyes is still happening in my life, and I hope it is still happening in yours. A passage of Scripture becomes open to me and I understand it, and I say, "Oh, that's really cool." Then I begin to see something important about the character of God in that Scripture and I see God in it. Whatever Scripture I read, I recognize God in there. To recognize someone, you have to know what they're like, and I'm seeing more about Him all the time. So that's how that applies.

Opening Our Minds to Apply

Now to the third opening. Cleopis and his friend returned to Jerusalem and were with the eleven.

> Luke 24:45 *Then he opened their minds, so that they could understand the Tanakh,*

I believe this is different from opening the Tanakh to them. This is opening their minds to it. I think there's a real difference in this. This means being able to make the leap from understanding the Scriptures to applying them to our own lives. That's a big leap. You may not think it is, but I think it is.

There are a lot of people who understand the Bible, but they don't actually live it. They don't apply it to their own lives. First, the Scriptures were opened to them so they could see that the Scriptures pointed to the Messiah. Then Yeshua opened their minds and applied it to their lives and commissioned them. After their minds were opened, He could say, "This applies to you guys. It applies to you because I'm sending you out."

Do you see? Before it was like, "Oh that's interesting. You were supposed to die and rise again. That's wonderful. We see that now." But then He says, "Wait a minute. Now I'm applying this to you. I'm opening your mind to see how this applies to you."

> Luke 24:47 *... and in his name repentance leading to forgiveness of sins is to be pro- claimed to people from all nations, starting with Yerushalayim (Jerusalem).*

He is commissioning them to go and proclaim the Good News. It is a direct call to action.

And so to go back to my story, in my life, my eyes were opened to the Scripture as I read John. I understood the Scriptures. I understood about Yeshua, who He was and that He was so wonderful, but my mind wasn't opened to the Scriptures. The Scriptures were opened to me, but my mind wasn't opened until I read the Sermon on the Mount in Matthew. That's when I understood that I had sinned, that I was among the "all" in Romans 3:23. (I didn't know that verse then yet, of course.)

> Romans 3:23 *since all have sinned and come short of earning God's praise.*

Reading the Sermon on the Mount was when I realized that I was a sinner. That's when I realized that I needed a way to pay the price for my own sin. That opening of the Scriptures to me was that now it was applying to my life. Before, it was just intellectual knowledge. "Oh yes, He rose from the dead. He fulfilled all these prophesies. Oh that's wonderful. He rose from the dead and He's still alive." You can have all of that, but how does that affect you?

That opening of my mind to the Scriptures showed me my need for His sacrifice, which finally brought me to the conclusion that I needed to take action about my situation. What was my action that was needed? I needed to repent! I hadn't even thought of that up to that moment. I was learning all this wonderful stuff from the Scriptures, and I was understanding them. But you see, my mind hadn't been opened to it to see how it applied to me.

So just to bring this along so that we don't think that this just applies to somebody getting saved. I think it applies to our walk continually with the Lord. After we've come to see Him and recognize Him, and we take action, after we've done the things that God wants us to do in that initial instance, then what happened in my life was there was this long list of things that my mind needed to be opened up to after that.

What kind of things am I talking about? Well, the reality of the supernatural, of the gifts of the Spirit actually still being around. Tithing. My mind had to be opened to tithing. It wasn't like that day after I got saved I started tithing. My mind had to be opened to that. Deliverance. The power over evil spirits, and that spirits could have influence on people. It took time. I had to be opened to that. The Messianic Movement. I had to be opened to be part of the Messianic Movement. Spiritual warfare, to going into the ministry, to how to lead people, how to confront people. All of those are things God had to work in me. But it wasn't like I was really open to them. It took time for my mind to be opened.

And looking back at the process that went on, it was the same process that we just saw in these two men. First of all, it started with the Holy Spirit lighting a fire in my spirit, making my heart desire to know if God was really in something that I had heard or read about. For instance, the Messianic Movement. I started to hear about this back in the early 1980s, and I wasn't really interested. I was very happy in the church that we were part of. People treated me well. It was like I was the token Jew and that was good. But I started hearing these things and my heart started to be quickened about it. Then the Holy Spirit opened my eyes to the Scriptures about these things through study and teachings, and prophetic words. In my case, God used Jonathan Bernis. I started to come and listen to his messages and started to see that God was saying something to me personally about this. The Spirit was opening the Scriptures to me.

Then the Spirit was opening my eyes to recognize that the Lord was in what Jonathan was saying. I recognized the Lord speaking through Jonathan. Do you see that? I recognized that God was involved in this thing called the Messianic Movement.

That makes me think of David Levine's testimony, our second rabbi here. He was standing in the back of our sanctuary during the worship service and he had a vision. He was in outer space looking back at the earth, and he was looking at the back of a man. And the man was saying, "Blessing on Zion. Blessing on Zion." And he prayed and asked God what all this was about, and he realized the man was God, and that God was pouring out His Spirit upon the Jewish people. Then a question was put to him. The question was, "Do you want to be a part of it?" David responded by leaving his job. He was a pastor in a local church. He came to our Messianic congregation without any offer of being on staff here, but just came because God was calling him to reach the Jewish people. God was in that. He recognized the Lord was in that.

I was one of the elders at the time. When David told us what he had done, we realized that the Lord was in that, and we hired him.

So the fourth opening is this opening of our eyes to see how these things apply to our lives, to say, "Oh this isn't just for intellectual understanding, but how does this apply to me? What are You calling me to do? What action are You calling me to take?"

Again to relate this to our involvement in the Messianic Movement. The Spirit said to my wife and I that we needed to start becoming part of the Shema Yisrael congregation, which involved a lot of changes in our lives. It involved, within a short time, selling a house and moving, our kids changing from one school to another, etc. God was calling us to action because the thing wasn't just intellectual understanding anymore. Now it was, "This has been revealed to you because I want you to do something."

So my questions to you are:

Do you want a fire of the Spirit in you?

Do you want the Scriptures to be opened to you?

Do you want your eyes be opened to see the Lord in the Scriptures?

And the fourth question. This is the tough one. Do you want your mind opened so God can apply the Scriptures to your life?

Okay. God saw you nodding your head and raising your hand.

So let's pray

Heavenly Father, we thank You that You rose from the dead. We thank You that You did it on one of your Appointed Times on First Fruits, and we thank You that You did that to remind us that we will rise also. We will rise from the dead. Thank you for revealing to us that You are alive right now. We pray, Father, that You would light a fire in our spirits. Help us to recognize when You're doing that, when we begin to have a passion about something, when we see an interest in something that that's Your spirit quickening that to us. We ask, Lord, that You would open Your Scriptures to us. We have had great revelations from You, Lord, but we know there's so much more. Give us more. Open our eyes to see You in the Scriptures, to see Your character, to come closer to You to understand You more, and to see whether it's You speaking to us in the Scriptures.

And finally, we ask You, Father, to open our minds to see what Your Scriptures are saying to us, to be able to apply what You have said to us, to be obedient, to step out. So we ask You, Father, refill us. This is especially appropriate when this is the same day when You breathed on Your talmidim and said, "Receive the Holy Spirit." Refill us.

[Raise up Your hands if you want to be refilled. We need to be refilled just like our gas tanks that need to be refilled every couple of days or our stomachs that need to be filled every day.]

Father, refill us. Refill us with Your Spirit. Let Your Spirit be alive in us. Quicken our spirits. Make our spirits be alive in You. We thank You, Father. In Yeshua's Name. Amen.

Chapter 6

His Resurrection Power Over Sin

What is God Trying to Teach us?

> Leviticus 23:11 ... *On the morrow after the Shabbat, the kohen is to wave it.*

We saw that the Shabbat being referred to here is the weekly Shabbat during the week of Unleavened Bread. So, now, we ask, what is the significance of this prophetically? And we've already learned the answer. What significant event in the life of Yeshua happened on the "morrow after the Shabbat," the Sunday during the week of Unleavened Bread? Say it again with me loud and clear, "The Resurrection!"

> John 20:1 *Early on the first day of the week, while it was still dark, Miryam from Magdala went to the tomb and saw that the stone had been removed from the tomb.*

As we learned earlier, that's when she saw that the tomb was empty. That Sunday, before the sun rose, was when Yeshua was resurrected from the dead. So the first thing is, His claim to being Messiah is strengthened by His rising from the dead at this Appointed Time of Firstfruits. He was crucified on Pesakh as the Lamb of God. He was the unleavened One without sin in His life and He fulfilled all those things about how the Matzah looks.

Then He rose from the dead on the next Appointed Time, on *Yom HaBikkurim,* Firstfruits. So we can see that God arranged all of this timing. But also as we've kept these Appointed Times over the years, we've come to understand that when God arranges these things on His calendar, He's usually trying to teach us something. There is something there about it that we are to learn.

When we come to Shavuot, we know that the Holy Spirit was given on that day, but in Judaism, they say that the Ten Commandments were given on that day, too. We see that as a very clear lesson that we need the Holy Spirit to understand Torah, and we need the Torah to walk in the Spirit. So we see deep teachings in the way and timing that God causes things to happen.

Why did God choose that Yeshua should rise from the dead on this day, on The Appointed Time of Firstfruits? To help us understand, appreciate, have faith in, and remember two things: first and foremost Yeshua's glorious, astounding Resurrection as the Firstfruits of those who will rise from the dead and secondly our resurrection as latter fruits at the fullness of His resurrection harvest.

Saved by His Life

There is something else though. This is where I want to really get into the meat of what I believe the Spirit wants us to grasp in this chapter. Why is it so important that we live with this reality that the Lord has resurrected. We've talked about one reason—proof that He is the one and only Messiah and Savior. But there are a couple of other interesting things that Rabbi Sha'ul says about this that are hard to understand.

We are going to look at them. This first one, we looked at before.

> 1 Corinthians 15:17 *and if the Messiah has not been raised, your trust is useless, and you are still in your sins.*

We learned that this phrase "you are still in your sins" is kind of shocking! He is saying, "Well, Messiah could have been sacrificed and His blood placed on the Cross and all that, but if He wasn't raised from the dead, you're still in your sins." That kind of shakes me up a little bit because I don't think most of us understood it that way. But thank the Lord, He did arise! Hallelujah!

Resurrection is the confirmation that Yeshua died, first of all. There are a couple of ways that this works out. Most importantly, the Resurrection is a confirmation that when Yeshua died, it was all part of God's plan and that Yeshua is our eternal, all-powerful, almighty Redeemer.

If He had simply died and not risen, then people would have said, "Well, He was an eloquent lunatic." Or they would say, "He was a deceiver and finally He died and that's the end of Him." But He arose!! Praise His Name!! This is why, if you read the Gospels, the religious leaders of His time were very adamant in taking great pains to make sure that nobody stole the body. Remember they even put a guard over the tomb to keep anyone from stealing the body because they knew if His body disappeared then everybody would say, "Wow! He rose from the dead! He really was the Messiah!" So that is one of the reasons. His resurrection is proof and confirmation.

But, being still "in your sins" means more. Rabbi Sha'ul speaks about this in another place.

> Romans 5:10 *For if when we were enemies we were reconciled to God through the death of His Son, much more, having <u>been</u> reconciled, we <u>shall be</u> saved by His life.*

Do you see what he is saying there? We are reconciled by His death, but we are saved by the fact that He is still alive, by His resurrection. So what is this all about? Everybody talks about His death being the thing that reconciles us and it is. That is what Sha'ul is saying: "having been reconciled to God" by His death on the Cross.

Here's how I understand it. It means that the forgiveness, the atonement for our sins—of the past, present, and future—was accomplished by His death. He died as the perfect sacrifice to atone for our sins. But if you read the Tanakh and some of the *Brit Khadashah,* New Covenant, you should understand that before Yeshua's sacrifice, people were reconciled to God by making the animal sacrifices and being repentant. David was reconciled to God.

One of the most telling verses in the New Covenant is in the story of the birth of Yochanan the Immerser (John the Baptist). Referring to Elizabeth and Zachariah, the Scripture says they "were righteous before God, observing all the mitzvot and ordinances of ADONAI blamelessly" (Luke 1:6). This was before the time of Yeshua. They were not sinless. It's not that they had never done anything wrong, but I am sure that when they did do something wrong, they brought sacrifices and repented, so then they were back in right standing with God. So before Yeshua's time it was possible to be righteous. But it wasn't possible to be "saved by His life" because He hadn't risen from the dead yet. Do you follow me so far?

We have received the Gospel, including the Resurrection. Sha'ul is saying, "We shall be saved by His life." His being still alive somehow saves us. What are we saved from by His life? If we are already forgiven and reconciled with God, what are we still needing to be saved from? It is really simple. It is right before our eyes. We are saved from the <u>ongoing power</u>

of sin in our lives, by the fact that He is still alive, and that we are able to have a relationship with Him. It is pretty simple, right? But it is very important because The Good News is more than just forgiveness for our sins. It also includes being saved from the deadly effects of sin in our lives really in two ways.

Saved from the Deadly Effects of My Sins

Here is the first way.

We are saved from reaping ruin and death for what we have sown to the flesh in the past.

> Galatians 6:7-8 *Don't delude yourselves: no one makes a fool of God! A person reaps what he sows. 8 Those who keep sowing in the field of their old nature, in order to meet its demands, will eventually reap ruin; but those who keep sowing in the field of the Spirit will reap from the Spirit everlasting life.*

I sowed lots of seeds to the flesh in the past and occasionally, I mess up and sow a seed to the flesh today. As I confess those things and as I receive the Lord's forgiveness and atonement for them, somehow I am saved by His life, by the fact that He is still alive.

Here is the second way. This is something that I think the Spirit wants us all to grasp.

We are save from reaping ruin and death for what we would sow to the flesh in the present and in the future that Galatians 6 speaks about. If God left us to our own devices, if we had to live this life with all the Word of God and all His instructions, but without the Spirit of God dwelling within us, without a relationship with Yeshua, we would be hopeless. I would be hopeless. Maybe you could do it, but I could never do it. If He wasn't resurrected and still alive, you see, we would be left on our own, in our own strength to deal with our flesh, to deal with our sinful nature, to deal with ha-satan. We would try to live our lives as best as we could in our natural wisdom, but we would be constantly getting ourselves in terrible trouble.

The only way we can continue to be "saved" from sin and bear fruit in our lives is by His <u>continued living</u> presence in our lives. So that's the other message here. Yeshua said this:

> John 15:4 *"Abide in Me, and I in you. As the branch cannot bear fruit of itself, unless it abides in the vine, neither can you, unless you abide in Me.*

So, abiding in Him, with His Spirit leading us at all times, following His leading and being obedient to His commandments, checking in with Him, not only for difficult moral decisions, but every day in all decisions. "What am I supposed to do today, Lord? Where am I supposed to go?" Making Him the one in charge of our lives is the only way we can live, not sowing to the flesh. We need Him to be in charge of our goals, our aspirations, our plans, our dreams, our purposes, all those things. His Word says that it is His living presence that enables us to live the life He created us for, and to keep you and me from re-enslavement to sin.

Being My Own Boss is Sin

So here's what I saw in studying this out, that I can believe that His death on the Cross was to forgive my sin and reconcile me to God, and to bring me eternal Life in Heaven. I can believe all that and still not walk with the Lord if I don't have that relationship with Him. If I'm trying to run my own life, everything I do is really sin. It's not obedience to God, so it is just sin because I am doing my own thing. So the reconciling death does me no good if I continue to be my own boss and my own lord. If I am not abiding in Him, I will continually be disobedient, and I will not bear any fruit, but will reap only ruin and death.

So salvation from continually messing up our lives is only possible through a living relationship with the Living Lord. And this is what the Old Testament saints didn't have. They knew God, the Father, but they didn't have a living relationship with the Living Messiah. If He hadn't risen, we would be like them. We would have sacrifices for our sins, but we wouldn't have that living relationship. We wouldn't have Him abiding in us

So, why was His Resurrection necessary? To save us from our sins through this living relationship. Now here's the punch line to the whole thing. Why couldn't it be any other way? We went over this before. You can't have a living relationship with a dead person. Really! There are lots of people in the occult who try to do that. You've probably read about that or seen it in movies where they try to bring people up from the dead. Right? That's what it would be! If Yeshua had not risen from the dead, and we went around telling people that the Lord speaks to me, people would be saying, "Oh really? You're communicating with the dead? You're a medium?" The Torah has commandments forbidding such things. The Bible teaches very strongly against attempting to communicate with a dead person. It is strictly forbidden.

So, it's only because Yeshua is forever alive that we can have this living relationship with Him, which provides ongoing salvation. And this is why it is power! It is real power! Resurrection Power!

Resurrection Power

The power is there because of the Resurrection. It is Resurrection Power! It provides our hope for the future. It is what gives us hope for our resurrection. It gives us hope that we can accomplish God's will, and that we can fulfill His purposes for us. So let's wrap up by looking at this verse where Sha'ul again speaks about this Resurrection Power being in you.

> Ephesians 1:18-20 *I pray that he will give light to the eyes of your hearts, so that you will understand the <u>hope</u> to which he has called you, <u>what rich glories there are in the inheritance he has promised his people.</u> 19 and how surpassingly great is his power working in us who trust him. It works with the same mighty strength he used 20 when he worked in the Messiah to <u>raise him from the dead</u>....*

So it's that same power of God that resurrected the Messiah that works in us. This is the hope that we need to keep in the forefront of our minds. We need to be reminded of it every year, on Resurrection Day, if not more often. When we have that power in us, the things of this world become less important. They become less of obstacles to us. We can keep things in perspective. We have this hope for our future. We have assurance of our victory over darkness. It's a yearly reminder of His promise of salvation. How? Let's say it together, through His Life. We are saved through His Life. I didn't make it up. You saw it. Rabbi Sha'ul wrote it. We are saved through His Life—through the fact that He is still alive.

Let's pray

Father, we are here before You today. I just thank You myself for understanding this. This has really touched my heart to understand the importance of that Living relationship with You. I've been taught it all the years that I have walked with You. People have spoken this to me that I have to have that relationship with the Living God, but when I see it now in those verses, it is so clear that not only do we need the relationship, but we are saved by that relationship. It's only in that relationship that we can hope to be pleasing servants to You, that we can walk with You and please You as Your children.

*****

I believe that you, dear reader, would like to have a closer relationship with the Lord. Am I right? Go ahead and nod your head or raise your hand if that is right. I don't think there is anyone who can say, "No, I don't need to come any closer. I've got it." Rabbi Sha'ul said this. "I strive toward knowing the Lord in a greater way." So lift your hands and pray this:

Lord, I want to know You better. I want a closer walk with You. I want a closer relationship with You. I want to experience Your Love. I want Your direction for my life. I submit my life to You, Lord. You are the Lord. I want to be saved by Your Life.

*****

We thank You, Father, for that reminder that it's by Your Life that we are saved. We agree together for our relationship with You to grow. We also thank You, Father, that You remind us at this time that there's going to be a future resurrection. Our bodies are aging. That's the way it is, and yet Your promises are that some day we are going to get a new one, and it's going to be an eternal one. And we want to remember that. We want to keep things in perspective that there are more important things that You have for us than this body and this life. Only You know what we are going to do with those new bodies. It could be all kinds of things.

So Father, I thank You today that we have this hope. I pray that as we move on in life, this hope for the future resurrection would sustain us and this understanding of our need to have that close relationship with You would give us the discipline, Lord, to come into Your presence every day and to spend that time with You, no matter what. Nothing is more important than standing in Your presence, abiding in the vine. We just thank You, Lord, that You love us so much that You want us to do this. In Yeshua's awesome Name. Amein. Amein.

Chapter 7

HIS RESURRECTION POWER OVER CURSES

Generational Curses

Have you ever wondered why the method of execution for Yeshua to be hung on the Cross? Well, the answer to that will reveal an important part of God's plan. It can only be understood with the knowledge of the Jewish practice at that time, which we will get to later.

First, let's get to the subject at hand, curses. In the last chapter, we saw that Yeshua's Resurrection Power gives us victory over our sin and keeps us from ruining our lives through our propensity to sin. It is a constant battle, over which Yeshua gives us victory.

But there are also things we struggle with that don't originate with our sin, namely curses which are mentioned in the first of the Ten Commandments

> Exodus 20:1 *Then God said all these words: 2 "I am ADONAI your God, who brought you out of the land of Egypt, out of the abode of slav-ery.3 "You are to have no other gods before me. 4 You are not to make for yourselves a carved image or any kind of representation of anything*

in heaven above, on the earth beneath or in the
water below the shoreline.

Some people think this is not applicable today because they don't worship statues. People do worship statues in Hinduism, Catholicism, Buddhism, though. What does this commandment really refer to? It is clear that idolatry is having other gods before the God of Israel, so, anything that is more important to you than the Lord is an idol. It could be money, job, success, person, spouse, parents, children, car, computer, music, sports, education, good causes, politics, philosophy, science, addictions, appearance, health, ministry, etc., can all be idols if we consider them more important than God.

> Exodus 20:5 *...I, ADONAI your God, am a jealous*
> *God, punishing the children for the sins of the*
> *parents to the third and fourth generation of those*
> *who hate me, 6 but displaying grace to the thou-*
> *sandth generation of those who love me and obey*
> *my mitzvot.*

God shows His grace to the thousandth generation of those who love Him, but punishes to the fourth generation those who hate Him. It says something very similar in Exodus 34

> Exodus 34:7 *Showing grace to the thousandth*
> *generation, forgiving offenses, crimes, and sins,*
> *yet not exonerating the guilty, but causing the*
> *negative effects of the parents' offenses to be*
> *experienced by their child*

Here it says that generational judgment is caused by sin rather than hatred of God. Note that His grace is for 1000 generations, which is 250 times longer than His justice.

These punishments are called generational curses because they come down from our ancestors

There are other curses that we bring on ourselves through disobedience, There's a long list of them in Deuteronomy 28. It doesn't take a Biblical scholar to point out that there are generational curses. We can see with our own natural eyes that children are affected by their parents' sin. We see it in the children of parents who were any of the following:

Abusive, alcoholic, addicted, adulterous, controlling, negligent, depressed, materialistic, covetous, complaining, gossiping.

These kinds of parents can scar their children. Is there a way to be set free from these? Not in the Mosaic Covenant –these were the just punishments that God decreed.

Deliverance From Curses

But, when God proclaimed the *Brit Khadashah* (New Covenant) to Jeremiah 600 years before the time of Yeshua, He said that it would bring a way to overcome these curses.

> Jeremiah 31:29-30 *"When those days come they will no longer say, 'The fathers have eaten sour grapes, and the children's teeth are set on edge.' 30 Rather, each will die for his own sin; every one who eats sour grapes, his own teeth will be set on edge.*

When those days come - punishment for sin will not be passed on to us from our parents and we won't pass them on to our children. But when will those days come?

> Jeremiah 31:31-34 *"Here, the days are coming,"* says ADONAI, *"when I will make a new covenant with the house of Isra'el and with the house of Y'hudah. ... "I will put my Law within them and write it on their hearts; I will be their God, and they will be my people. 34 No longer will any of them teach his fellow community member or his brother, 'Know ADONAI'; for all will know me, from*

*the least of them to the greatest; because I will
forgive their iniquity and remember their sins no
more."*

Why the Cross?

Yeshua came and fulfilled this awesome promise of the Brit Khadashah by dying a sacrificial death to pay the price for our sins, and by being bruised to bear our iniquities. But He died in a very specific way to deal with the curses we are subject to due to our own sin and our ancestors' sins.

> Galatians 3:13 *The Messiah redeemed us from
> the curse pronounced in the Torah by becom-
> ing cursed on our behalf; for the Tanakh says,
> "Everyone who hangs from a stake comes under
> a curse."*

Paul was quoting this verse.

> Deuteronomy 21:22-23 *If someone has commit-
> ted a capital crime and is put to death, then hung
> on a tree, 23 his body is not to remain all night
> on the tree, but you must bury him the same day,
> because a person who has been hanged has
> been cursed by God -so that you will not defile
> your land, which ADONAI your God is giving you
> to inherit.*

The reason Yeshua's method of execution had to be crucifixion was to take upon Himself the curses the Law of God declares are to be on us for our own sin, for the sins of our ancestors, and for some other curses we'll talk about later.

Now again, Yeshua taking our curses upon Himself by being hung on the Cross would have no power at all for us if He hadn't risen from the dead. So the power we have over curses is both from His Cross and His Resurrection. It is Resurrection Power.

This goes along with the understanding of the power of Yeshua's atonement in being:

- wounded for transgression
- striped/whipped for our healing
- bruised for iniquity
- rejected for our acceptance
- resurrected for our life

In the same way He allowed Himself to be whipped to bring physical healing to us who trust in Him, He died specifically on a cross or tree to enable curses to be broken in our lives. Power in His Resurrection because of the Cross.

But, here's where an understanding of Jewish customs comes in. Being hung on a tree has never been a Jewish means of execution. Jewish people executed people by stoning or sword. On very rare occasion, the bodies of those put to death were then hung on trees. So why would the Jewish Messiah die in a totally un-Jewish way? Paul answers this question in the next verse

> *Galatians 3:14 Yeshua the Messiah did this so*
> *that in union with him the Gentiles might receive*
> *the blessing announced to Avraham, so that*
> *through trusting and being faithful, we might re-*
> *ceive what was promised, namely, the Spirit.*

Galatians is primarily written to Gentiles, and here Paul specifically says this curse breaking is for the benefit of the Gentiles. Why did the Gentiles particularly need curses broken more than Jews? Well many Jews had parents, grandparents & great grandparents who were lovers of God, and keepers of Torah. As I pointed out earlier, Luke tells us about two of these, Z'charyah & Elisheva, the parents of John the Immerser (Baptist) were such people.

Luke 1:6 Both of them were righteous before
God, observing all the mitzvot and ordinances of
ADONAI blamelessly.

So John would have been free of generational curses. But there was no hope for Gentiles to escape those curses because their ancestors would not have kept God's law. They would've worshipped other God's and possibly even hated the Lord. This is why Yeshua had to be executed in a Gentile way, and not a Jewish way commanded by God in Torah, or from Jewish culture. So for many years in the beginning of the church, the generational curses would have been mostly on Gentiles, but this is not necessarily so today when so many Jewish people have turned away from obeying Torah.

How does Yeshua's crucifixion becoming a curse on our behalf work? Does it happen automatically when person is born from above? Some think it does, I don't.

I had to deal with reaping much destruction I had personally sown. But I also had to deal with the effects of curses from my parents and grandparents on my father's side who didn't keep Torah and definitely hated God! I went through lots of deliverance from these curses.

For example, my parents were communists and didn't believe in capitalism. They didn't believe in earning money by making investments. After I was grown and on my own, I had great difficulty saving money or understanding how to invest money I received. One day I began to realize this came from my parents and broke that curse, and things changed.

Later we're going to pray to break curses in your life.

Another Kind of Curse

Now I want to address another kind of curse that has been largely ignored in the Body of Messiah. There is a vivid example of it in Scripture. After Israel came out of slavery in Egypt, they had to travel through Mo'av (Moab). When the people of Mo'av saw them coming, they were in great fear, so Balak, the King of Mo'av, sent a message to a Bil'am (Balaam), asking him to curse Israel. Bil'am had spiritual power, but was forbidden by the Lord to curse Israel and ended up blessing them.

Based on this story some believe that a curse against a believer by another person is not possible.

> Proverbs 26:2 (NKJV) *Like a flitting sparrow, like a flying swallow, So a curse without cause shall not alight.*

But, notice it says *"a curse without a cause,"* an undeserved curse. But, there may be things in our lives that allow curses to come home to roost. It could be generational. It could be that our own sin opens a door for it. If we read further in the story of Bil'am, he did manage to bring a curse on Israel.

> Numbers 31:16 *...because of Bil'am's advice -caused the people of Isra'el to rebel, breaking faith with ADONAI in the P'or incident, so that the plague broke out among ADONAI's community!*

What happened in that rebellion? It occurred just after Bil'am gave up. In Numbers 25:1-4 you can read how the women of Mo'av enticed the Israelite men into worshipping their gods, and so brought the anger of the Lord upon Israel. The leaders who fell into this sin were to be hanged on trees after they died, which is the same punishment for those who were cursed. Twenty-four thousand people died in the plague that followed. So, Bil'am managed to bring a curse on Israel through his advice rather than by his spell casting.

******

There are many more very important points and much more detailed instructions about breaking curses in your life in my *Yom Kippur* book in chapters 11 and 12. It includes personal stories about our experiences in our congregation of breaking curses that had been spoken against us by those apposed to the Messianic Movement.

Let's Pray

Thank You, Father, for being a God of justice. We see that we reap what we sow, both good and evil. Show us the evil we have sown. We repent of it and ask You to cover it with the Blood of Messiah that we might stop reaping ruin from it.

Thank You for redeeming us from the curse pronounced in the Torah by becoming a curse on our behalf to break curses we've brought on ourselves through our own disobedience and through our ancestors.

We break curses we are under due to the sin of our ancestors. Reveal those curses to us. We ask you to redeem us from those curses. Break them according to your promise of becoming a curse for us

Thank you for revealing that some of those who oppose us and our ministry work have spoken curses against us. We break those curses by the same redeeming power of Messiah who became a curse for us. And we speak blessing on those who have cursed us. We pray that they will come to know You, Yeshua, as their Messiah.

Chapter 8

RESURRECTION POWER to FORGIVE

Indroduction

Yeshua appeared to His talmidim after His resurrection.

> *John 20:19-23 In the evening that same day, the first day of the week, when the talmidim were gathered together behind locked doors out of fear of the Judeans, Yeshua came, stood in the middle and said, "Shalom aleikhem!" 20 Having greeted them, he showed them his hands and his side. The talmidim were overjoyed to see the Lord. 21 "Shalom aleikhem!" Yeshua repeated. "Just as the Father sent me, I myself am also sending you." 22 Having said this, he breathed on them and said to them, "Receive the Ruach HaKodesh! 23 If you forgive someone's sins, their sins are forgiven; if you hold them, they are held."*

I will discuss Yeshua's breathing on them to receive the Ruach HaKodesh (verse 22) in Chapter 9. In this chapter, we'll look at His statement on forgiveness (verse 23).

It is significant that the first thing Yeshua told His talmidim to do after receiving the Ruach HaKodesh was to forgive. The significance of the timing shows us the great importance to the Lord of forgiveness. Not our forgiveness by Him, which of course is very important, but our forgiveness of others. So, Yeshua's instruction to us on forgiveness of others was a very important part of His Resurrection Day.

There is a power in Yeshua's resurrection we usually ignore or don't even realize is there. It was revealed to me several years ago and was triggered by something that I heard. I just want to share this with you. It is about forgiveness and is so good.

We all like to focus on His Resurrection Power that gives us authority and power over ha-satan and all his evil spirits and power to pray for healing, and for mighty miracles, which is wonderful and great and very important, and we will focus on that later. But His power over unforgiveness in our hearts that also comes from His Resurrection is actually of first importance because it is what we need to focus on first. Otherwise, we will see too little of the other mighty manifestations of His Resurrection Power in our lives. If we do focus on His power to forgive first, then we will see more and better results in all the other power and authority we have in His Resurrection.

During the week after this power for forgiveness was revealed to me, a couple of people came to me and said that they were struggling with forgiving someone. That was the way the Holy Spirit spoke to me to give a sermon about forgiveness and to focus on it in this chapter.

Before we even start, I want you to agree with me in prayer in binding the spirit of unforgiveness because unforgiveness is a spirit. So we want to bind that spirit right away to prevent anybody from not being able to understand as they read this.

Let's Pray

Father, if any time we are in unforgiveness, we ask forgiveness for that, Lord. In the Name of Yeshua, in the authority that was given to us by His Name, we bind the power of the spirit of unforgiveness to keep us from hearing the Word of God and what the Spirit of God is saying to us. In the Name of Yeshua, we pray. Amen.

Unforgiveness Test

Okay, with that spirit bound, I'd like to propose a little test for you. So close your eyes and imagine you're at a place where you are looking forward to having a great time of fellowship. Your best friends are there, and maybe family members that you really love and it's going to be great. There are going to be games. It's going to be fun. There will be all kinds of love there. Who would you not want to see at the door? Who comes to your mind that would take away all your excitement, that would hamper the whole thing and make you not look forward to it? Who would that be in your life? It might be more than one person for you.

That's just a little bit of a test to make all of us realize that we probably need to hear something about forgiveness. There's probably someone that you might need to forgive. Right?

Unforgiveness is the first step down the road to bitterness. We don't want to go down that road. So we're going to chop unforgiveness off at that first step today.

How Important is Forgiving Others?

I'm going to start with something that is so familiar to all of us, but it might be a surprise to you what comes after it. It will lead to the revelation I just mentioned.

> Matthew 6:9-13 (KJV) *Our Father which art in heaven, Hallowed be thy name. 10 Thy kingdom come. Thy will be done in earth, as it is in heaven. 11 Give us this day our daily bread. 12 And forgive us our debts, as we forgive our debtors. 13 And lead us not into temptation, but deliver us from evil: For thine is the kingdom, and the power, and the glory, for ever. Amen.*

That's the Lord's prayer. You know it by heart, right? But do you know what comes right after it, in the very next sentence?

> Matthew 6:14-15 *For if you forgive others their offenses, your heavenly Father will also forgive you; 15 but if you do not forgive others their offenses, your heavenly Father will not forgive yours.*

Did you know that was what follows right after the Lord's prayer? I'm guessing not because most people don't. I didn't realize it myself.

Now just to understand a little bit more about this part, *"forgive us our debts as we forgive our debtors"* for anybody who might be confused and think it is about finances. The Greek there is *ofalama* and it means *that which is owed,* but it also means *an offense, a sin, or a trespass.* Debtors in this prayer are those who owe us something because they have wronged us. One thing they owe us, obviously, is an apology, but they might also owe us retribution. Other translations of the Lord's Prayer will say those who have transgressed against us, or those who have sinned against us, or those who have offended us.

Now the Lord's Prayer really should be called the disciples' prayer because it was what He told the disciples to pray. It was His instructions. It wasn't a rote prayer to be recited over and over again. It was an example of how to pray. He was teaching them about prayer.

So here *"forgive us our debts as we forgive our debtors,"* seems like He is teaching that as we forgive others, God will forgive us. In other words if we forgive all the sins of others, God will forgive all our sins, but if we forgive less than all, then He will forgive less than all of our sins.

So notice that these two verses, 14 and 15, that come immediately after the Lord's/Disciples' Prayer, are if-then statements. The if-then statements are commands that emphasize this further. If you forgive others their offenses what happens? God will forgive yours. If you don't forgive them what happens? God will not forgive yours. Notice that this command is continuing Yeshua's teaching on how to pray. In other words, He's saying, "I'd better make sure you're forgiving everybody before you try to pray to God because it's vitally important. You're spiritual survival depends on it!" It actually is the inverse of what Yeshua said just a few verses earlier.

> *Matthew 5:23 So if you are offering your gift at the Temple altar and you remember there that your brother has something against you,*

Now why would someone have something against you? Well, maybe you criticized them, cheated them, lied to them, judged them, gossiped about them, did something to hurt them. The Ruakh HaKodesh, Holy Spirit will reveal to us what we've done and will convict us. When He does reveal some such thing, what are we supposed to do?

> *Matthew 5:24 leave your gift where it is by the altar, and go, make peace with your brother. Then come back and offer your gift.*

So here it's if someone else has something against me. It's saying don't even try to worship. Go make peace, then come back. Reconcile, apologize. Then God will receive my worship.

Verses 14 through 15 in Matthew 6 say the inverse. Can you see this? Let's look at those two verses again.

> Matthew 6:14-15 *For if you forgive others their offenses, your heavenly Father will also forgive you; 15 but if you do not forgive others their offenses, your heavenly Father will not forgive yours.*

In Matthew chapter 5, it's talking about finding other people that you have wronged, and you've got to straighten things out with them. Then in Matthew chapter 6 it's about other people offending you and you've got to straighten that out by forgiving them. So there's no escape. There's no place to hide. Either way, it has to be taken care of. Either way, we have the responsibility. It looks like our salvation depends on it!

Wait! What?

You know, as I thought about it, this is really significant because these two verses have a huge impact, a twist really, on our understanding of salvation. Salvation means God forgives our sins. Right? So when we trust in the Lord Yeshua's sacrifice to pay the penalty for our sins, we're saved and we're forgiven. Right? Right! But according to these two verses, even if we put our trust in Yeshua, there's another requirement for our sins to be forgiven. Our sins will only be forgiven if what? If we forgive others! So we could say if we're walking in unforgiveness, we're not saved!! Whoa! I don't know about you, but that shakes me to the core!

Why Is Forgiving Others So Important?

Hang onto your boots. Let's look at why. Why is forgiving others so important to God? It's best explained by Yeshua Himself when Peter asked Him about forgiving.

> Matthew 18:21 *Then Kefa (Peter) came up and said to him, "Rabbi, how often can my brother sin against me and I have to forgive him? As many as seven times?"*

Many people have this question. "Do I have to keep forgiving someone if they keep doing the same thing over and over again?" Now this question from Kefa was prompted by what Yeshua was teaching about conflict resolution. That's what Matthew 18 is all about. Yeshua says to go to your brother if he has offended you and confront him. Here's Yeshua's answer.

> Matthew 18:22 *"No, not seven times," answered Yeshua, "but seventy times seven!*

That's 490 times! So, unless you are going to keep running tabs on everyone on your phone, letting it keep track for you... Actually, that wouldn't be right because I Corinthians 13:5 says "Love keeps no record of wrongs." So based on the verses above that we read, that if we don't forgive, God won't forgive us, my interpretation here is that He means you always have to forgive. You always have to forgive those who sin against you.

Yeshua's Parable Explains it all

Then Yeshua gives us an incredible parable to explain why, and if you don't grasp this parable, you're really missing the whole point of the Bible. It's incredible when you see what it's saying!

> Matthew 18:23 *Because of this, the Kingdom of Heaven may be compared with a king who decided to settle accounts with his deputies.*

In this parable, the king is Father God and the deputies (or servants as in other translations) are you and I.

> Matthew 18:24 *Right away they brought forward a man who owed him many millions;*

That's in David Stern's translation, but in the Greek it says ten thousand talents, and if you want to go to Google and look up how much a talent is worth, it's more than a million dollars! So, if a talent is worth a million dollars the servant's debt was ten billion dollars!

Now I believe Yeshua purposely chose an enormous amount for a reason. He wants to drive home the point of this parable, and it's about the fact of how big that debt is. The servant's ten thousand talents represents the value of what you and I owe from a lifetime of sin, a lifetime of falling short. (Remember, in the Hebrew the word for sin, khata'a חטא, means falling short of God's standards.) And it's what we owe from a lifetime of transgressions, pesha פֶּשַׁע, which is actually breaking the laws of Torah on purpose, knowing you are doing wrong, but doing it anyway, and also a lifetime of iniquity, avone עָוֹן, which is our flesh rising up. So it includes all of our sins in behavior, in speech, and in thought—all of that.

Now you might be thinking, "That doesn't make sense. Why would I owe so much?" Well, if you know God's Word, you know it's difficult to live up to His standards, His Word, at all times. Really! We recite this one every Shabbat: *You shall love the Lord your God with all your heart all your soul and all your strength.* Who amongst us can say everything we did today was done out of love for God? We also recite this one: *Love your neighbor as yourself.* Who can say you've loved your neighbor more than yourself all day today or yesterday? Then in Exodus 20, this is the one that always gets me.

> Exodus 20:3 *You shall have no other gods before Me.*

This is the first of the Ten Commandments and *"before Me"* means more important than God. So what other gods could you have that would be more important than God to you today? I don't think there's a single person reading this book who has gotten down on their knees this morning and prayed in front of a statue. You haven't, right? But what things have taken priority in your life over God today or yesterday? Pride, anger, fear, greed, bitterness, self-pity, envy, impressing others? Lust? Who amongst us can say, "Nothing has been more important to me than God is," even just today?

Who can say. "I've considered others better than myself all day today"? Who can say, "I've taken up my cross and followed Yeshua every day"? Who can say they haven't gossiped, coveted, doubted, or judged in the last week? I don't see your hand. You won't see my hand either.

Suppose you fell short in just one of those things per day and lived to be 70 years old. Do the arithmetic. That would be twenty-five thousand five hundred and fifty (25,550) sins in a lifetime. Now, in addition, you owe God for giving you life! The air we breathe! The abilities you have! The family that took care of you; the love that you experienced from people. You owe Him for all that!

Now, because God is a God of justice, the penalty must be paid for every violation of His Word. That's your debt! That's your debt in the sense that you owe Him the penalty for all of your sins, all of your violations. So how much would that be? What would the fine be if you had to pay a fine for every one of those twenty-five thousand five hundred fifty violations? Well, a parking ticket in my city at minimum is $40. So I did the math. One million, twenty-two thousand dollars ($1,022,000.00) would be what you owe!

But there's good news. Yeshua took your sins and my sins upon Himself, and He paid your debt by suffering and dying for you on the Cross. Yes, you can applaud and praise Him for that!!! Hallelujah!!! We thank You, Yeshua! We praise You! We can never thank You and praise You enough for this alone!!!

So the point is, and this is really the whole point of the whole parable. God has forgiven you a very huge, enormous, gigantic debt, just like the king in this parable forgave the huge debt his servant owed him. So let's look at how he does that.

> Matthew 18:25 *and since he couldn't pay, his master ordered that he, his wife, his children and all his possessions be sold to pay the debt.*

He was going to be sold into slavery. Back in those days, that's the way debts were dealt with. Really they were dealt with that way from Biblical times until the late 1800s. In the late 1800s slavery was abolished and the modern bankruptcy laws that we have today came into effect. So it wasn't that long ago that debtors were sold into slavery.

> Matthew 18:26 *But the servant fell down before him. "Be patient with me," he begged, "and I will pay back everything." 27 So out of pity for him, the master let him go and forgave the debt.*

So the king forgave him twenty billion dollars! There's no way the servant could have paid back that debt. So I hope you get it now. God forgave you and I a similar debt by counting Yeshua's sacrifice as payment for our debt, which was way beyond what you or I could ever pay. And why did God do it? It says it in the verse. What's the word? Compassion, pity—for love! That was God's motivation for giving you forgiveness. Let's go on.

> Matthew 18:28 *But as that servant was leaving, he came upon one of his fellow servants who owed him some tiny sum. He grabbed him and*

*began to choke him, crying, "Pay back what you
owe me!"*

Now David Stern translates this as *"tiny sum."* It's actually
a hundred denarii. That's not that small of a sum. Let's do the
arithmetic. Assuming about ten dollars an hour is minimum
wage, a Denari would be worth about eighty dollars. So we're
talking about eight thousand dollars $8,000. It's a sizable sum.
You can see why he grabbed him, but what is it compared to
twenty billion dollars that he had just been forgiven? It's tiny
compared to that.

Matthew 18:29 *His fellow servant fell before him
and begged, "Be patient with me, and I will pay
you back."*

Actually that wasn't unreasonable. A hundred days of
work would have paid this lender back, well more, maybe 200
or 300 days depending on his living expenses, but doable. It
was nothing like what the king's servant owed the king. So
the point here, have you got it? The point is the ways we've
sinned against each other, the ways we have offended each
other are tiny compared to the ways in which we have sinned
against God and offended God. Can you see that? We see
it in our intellect, yes. But we've got to know it deep in our
heart, so that it comes out in our thoughts and words and
actions. That's the point.

Matthew 18:30 *But he refused; instead, he had
him thrown in jail until he should repay the debt.*

He didn't even sell him into slavery to pay the debt. He
threw him in jail so he couldn't pay! The king's servant was
just one mean guy, basically.

Matthew 18:31 *When the other servants saw what
had happened, they were extremely distressed;
and they went and told their master everything
that had taken place.*

These servants knew their king had forgiven his servant an enormous amount!

> Matthew 18:32 Then the master summoned his servant and said, "You wicked servant! I forgave you all that debt just because you begged me to do it."

The king knew he was wicked. He calls him wicked. This next verse is so important.

> Matthew 18:33 *"Shouldn't you have had pity on your fellow servant, just as I had pity on you?"*

Shouldn't you have as much compassion on those who sin against you as God has had mercy on you? That's speaking to each of us. How much compassion did He have on you? He forgave your lifetime of sin.

> Matthew 18:34 *And in anger his master turned him over to the jailers for punishment until he paid back everything he owed.*

So what's the point? Because God has forgiven you, it's very important to Him that you forgive others. Do you see that? If you don't forgive others, it's actually a sign to God that you don't appreciate; you don't understand; you don't value how merciful He's been to you. You haven't grasped it.

Now how long will the king's servant be punished? In case you're wondering about your own case, whether you can ever be forgiven again once you've not forgiven someone. How long will he be punished? Well, when I first looked at this, my first thought was he'll be punished until he can pay back the twenty billion! But that's not it. That debt had already been forgiven. So legally the king could not claim it again. Right? He had promised! He had forgiven him the whole twenty billion!

The Sin of Unforgiveness

So what did the king's servant still owe? The twenty billion had been wiped away. He now owed the king for the sin of unforgiveness, which he had just committed by grabbing that other servant and throwing him in jail. Because he had received such great forgiveness from the king, he owed forgiveness to others who were in debt to him. Do you see the Kingdom economic system? This is like God's economy. It's the way God has His Kingdom set up. This is His banking system. If that wicked servant forgave the debts of all those who owed him, he'd be released from prison. See that? Because that's all he owed. And then this next verse really pierces.

> Matthew 18:35 *This is how my Heavenly Father will treat you unless you each forgive your brother from your hearts.*

Therefore if we don't forgive, you and I will also be turned over to the jailers for punishment. Who are the jailers? They are demons. They are satanic spirits that will have a legal right to torment us, to make things difficult for us because we have not forgiven.

So even though you have been forgiven by God for a life time of sin against Him, if you don't forgive those who've sinned against you, you will basically be turned over to ha-satan's power for punishment! Whoa!! That's heavy!

But once you do forgive those who have sinned against you, your punishment will end and you will be released.

We all struggle with trials in our lives. Have you had trials in your life? Yes? Have you considered that perhaps some of the trials you're experiencing are because you haven't forgiven all those who have offended you? Could be.

How? When Emotions Are So Strong?

Now let's get to the practical side. How can you forgive when emotions like resentment, hatred, retaliation, and bitterness rise up when you even just think about certain people? You imagined that scene and you saw somebody's face walking in the room, and you're groaning, "Ugh!" How can you forgive that person?

Well, certainly by receiving this message and obeying these passages that we've just read, but also realizing that forgiving is not an emotion. It is not an emotion, it is an act of obedience. Warm feelings toward that person that you forgive may come, or they may never come. It's not about your feelings. What is sure to come, though, is the result of God's promise, which is really big! Do you see that? The promise that God will forgive you.

Notice that the word there in some translations is trespass. *"For if you forgive others their trespasses, your heavenly Father will also forgive you...."* (NRSV) Trespass is pesha. It is intentional wrongdoing. When you trespass against a person, it means, "I know I shouldn't do this to this person, but I'm going to do it anyway," which makes it a really serious offense. So Yeshua is saying, if we forgive others even what they do intentionally against us, God will forgive us.

So no matter how you feel, you can forgive. You have to simply make a decision to obey. Exercise your free will, which you have and carry out that decision, and obey.

Rabbi Sha'ul talks about this.

> Romans 12:19 *Never seek revenge, my friends; instead, leave that to God's anger; for in the Tanakh it is written, "ADONAI says, 'Vengeance is my responsibility; I will repay.'"*

You are standing in the way of God dealing with the person who sinned against you by holding that against him.

Romans 12:20 *On the contrary, "If your enemy is hungry, feed him; if he is thirsty, give him something to drink. For by doing this, you will heap fiery coals [of shame] on his head."*

In David Stern's translation, he put in brackets "[of shame]." It means the shame of conviction by the Holy Spirit. By doing acts of kindness, you'll make your enemy ashamed of what he or she has done to you. And also we should include a prayer. Praying for the people who've offended you is a way of heaping fiery coals on them, in other words, releasing them to experience the conviction of the Ruakh HaKodesh.

So let me tell you some of the ways that I've found to help me to forgive. One of them is obviously obedience and setting your will, but here's another one. It is based on this verse. Yeshua is speaking to the Father.

John 17:23 *I united with them and you with me, so that they may be completely one, and the world thus realize that you sent me, and that you have loved them just as you have loved me.*

This is amazing phrasing, *that You have loved them just as You have loved Me.* So if the person who you are having trouble forgiving is a believer, grasping this verse tells you that God loves that person as much as He loves Yeshua. Think about that person as someone whom Yeshua loves.

If that person is not a believer, do you have to forgive them, too? Let's see.

Romans 5:8 *But God demonstrates his own love for us in that the Messiah died on our behalf while we were still sinners.*

So if you're not forgiving someone who is not a believer, you're not forgiving someone whom God loves.

It's An Unclean Spirit

I've counseled many who are struggling to forgive someone, even when they understand God's commands, and, as I mentioned above, the price they pay for holding on to unforgiveness is horribly high. So I've concluded that unforgiveness is a demonic spirit. That's why we started out by binding that spirit.

So if you're having trouble forgiving someone even though you know God commands it, understand that unforgiveness is a spirit, and the way we deal with spirits is two steps. We repent of going along with them however long we've done that, right? Because if you've been in a place of unforgiveness toward a person for a while, that means that unclean spirit has had power over you! You are doing what it wants! So you need to repent of the unforgiveness, and then you renounce that spirit and command it to leave in Yeshua's Name. Then you might find you're able to forgive.

Who Else Do We Need To Forgive?

Now another aspect of this is that when people deal with unforgiveness, it's usually toward other people. Right? But many struggle with unforgiveness toward three other beings. The first one is God. Why would you need to forgive God? Well, some people, and maybe someone reading this book, blame God for everything they don't like about their lives or about themselves. They blame God for their looks, for their lack of ability in certain areas, for their dysfunctions, for their handicaps, for the circumstances of their lives, and for whatever trials they've experienced, whatever traumas they've experienced, and whatever losses they've experienced. They blame God for all those things. They blame God for being born into the family they were born into because it was dysfunctional. They blame God for the neighborhood they grew up in because it was tough, and they got beat up pretty bad. They blame God for the school that they went to because they didn't teach them well. Their unforgiveness towards God is the source of their bitterness towards God and it blocks their ability to love Him and experience His love.

The second being that people struggle to forgive is themselves. Have you forgiven yourself for your failures? For your fears? For the times when you gave in to evil, for anger and pride and greed, and lust that's gotten you into trouble? Unforgiveness of yourself leads to self bitterness which causes many different diseases and malfunctions. I have to do a lot of forgiving of myself for some things I did B.Y. (before Yeshua), and some things A.Y. (after Yeshua)!

And then finally, the third being is someone who is no longer with us. Have you forgiven those who died who hurt you or offended you? They don't need to be alive for the poison of unforgiveness to work on you. If you're still holding it against them, you are being poisoned. I saw this phrase once. I love it. It says this, "Not forgiving is like drinking poison expecting it to harm your enemy."

How in Real Practice?

Now let's look at the other side again.

> Matthew 18:21-22 *Then Kefa came up and said to him, "Rabbi, how often can my brother sin against me and I have to forgive him? As many as seven times?" 22 "No, not seven times," answered Yeshua, "but seventy times seven!*

Do you know what's missing in those two verses? There's no mention of an apology being needed for me to forgive. Right? An apology helps. Absolutely! If somebody has apologized to you, but you still can't forgive them, then you have problems. You might really be like that king's unforgiving servant in the parable. But maybe the person hasn't apologized, so you're still hanging on to the unforgiveness. You're still drinking the poison because they haven't apologized.

But we're not forgiving for their sake, right? We're forgiving for our own sake, so that God will forgive us. So sometimes we have to forgive without an apology.

> Matthew 5:24 *leave your gift where it is by the altar, and go, make peace with your brother. Then come back and offer your gift.*

If you want to worship God, that's what it is saying here, "leave your gift at the altar." So if you want to worship God, you have to make an attempt to reconcile if they have something against you, rightly or wrongly (whether you really did anything wrong or not), and/or if you have something against them. Now there have been times in my life, and I'm sure in yours, where you attempt to reconcile and what happens? It doesn't work. But you've done your part, as the prophets would say, the blood is off your hands.

Sometimes a person might know you have been offended by them and they still don't apologize. When you forgive them, you don't need to tell them at all. Definitely don't say, "Oh, now I've forgiven you for the terrible things you did." No, don't do that! That would only cause more trouble. Just do something to show that you're okay with them. Give them a smile, a card, a gift, a kind word. If the person knows you have been offended by them, then after you've forgiven them, you may have to lovingly confront them to get them to change their behavior and not do it again. But make sure it is done gently with your heart full of love.

Boundaries

Now here's something that everybody struggles with. Does forgiving mean you have to trust that person who hurt you? No! You don't have to expose yourself to being hurt again. Absolutely not! Trust is earned over time. You can have boundaries after forgiving. You can say, "I forgive you, but I'm not having you over to my house." That's fine. Or "I'm not hanging out with you, but you're forgiven."

How about if you are aware someone is offended at you? How should you apologize? Well, I have to say that people don't know how to apologize. I've seen it happen over and over again. The three sentences are: "I'm sorry. What I did or said was wrong. Please forgive me." Pretty simple, right? But it isn't, because people almost always add buts to shift the blame off themselves, like, "I'm sorry but I was really upset because of what you did." That's not an apology. Or, "I'm sorry, but if you hadn't done that to me, I wouldn't have done what I did to you." Or here's one that goes way back to Genesis, "But the devil made me do it." or "So-and-so made me do it."

So that's what the Holy Spirit wanted to challenge you with in this chapter. And as I was praying about how to wrap this up, I got a very clear message that we should come to the Sudat Adonai, the Lord's Table with this as the subject. So that is what we will do in the next chapter.

Let's Pray

Father, I take responsibility for the times when I've given in to unforgiveness, to resentment, to some retaliation, to hatred, to bitterness; the times I've given in to evil thoughts, words, or deeds. I repent of going along with those spirits, and now in the Name of Yeshua, I break the power of unforgiveness, of resentment, of retaliation, of anger, of hatred, of bitterness, of pride over me. I break all that power over me right now in the Name of Yeshua.

And we ask, Father, [and I hope you could be agreeing with me because we're going to have a minute here to do this], we ask You to examine our hearts.

*****

Now, spend some time in silence before the Lord, and ask Him through His Ruakh, His Spirit to speak to you and reveal to you any trace of unforgiveness in your heart. And ask Him for the courage to be obedient and deal with it all.

The next chapter will help you more in examining yourself to be ready for partaking from His Communion Table, the Sudat Adonai.

Chapter 9

HIS RESURRECTION POWER IN SUDAT ADONAI/ COMMUNION

Quick First Reading of the Verses

So I'm just going to read some of the verses in 1 Corinthians 11 about coming to the Sudat Adonai. We will go through these verses in much more detail later, but let's just look at them quickly right now.

> I Corinthians 11:23 *For what I received from the Lord is just what I passed on to you - that the Lord Yeshua, on the night he was betrayed, took bread;* 24 *and after he had made the b'rakhah he broke it and said, "This is my body, which is for you. Do this as a memorial to me";*

So Yeshua declared the Matzah a memorial to remember His physical body. Why His physical body? Because that was what was sacrificed for you to pay the penalty for your sin.

> I Corinthians 11:25 *likewise also the cup after the meal, saying, "This cup is the New Covenant effected by my blood; do this, as often as you drink it, as a memorial to me."*

And He declared that cup of wine or grape juice a memorial of His Blood that was shed to seal the New Covenant by which we have the Lord's forgiveness.

> I Corinthians 11:26-31 *For as often as you eat this bread and drink the cup, you proclaim the death of the Lord, until he comes. 27 Therefore, whoever eats the Lord's bread or drinks the Lord's cup in an unworthy manner will be guilty of dese-crating the body and blood of the Lord! 28 So let a person examine himself first, and then he may eat of the bread and drink from the cup; 29 for a person who eats and drinks without recognizing the body eats and drinks judgment upon himself. 30 This is why many among you are weak and sick, and some have died! 31 If we would examine our-selves, we would not come under judgment.*

Principality of Bitterness

So the Ruakh, the Spirit of God is telling each of us to examine ourselves. He wants to reveal any unforgiveness that you are carrying or anything that has developed into resentment, even thoughts of retaliation—how to get back at them, or just plain outright hatred or anything like that. All of those things are like unclean spirits and they are all under a principality of ha-satan. That principality is bitterness. They all lead to bitterness. Bitterness is a terrible thing. It separates us from God and causes all kinds of diseases. When you go to bed angry, you wake up with what? Bitterness. So forgiveness is very important. We must forgive or lovingly confront, or bitterness will come and overpower us. And we may need to apologize to someone.

The unclean spirit of bitterness tries to make it hard for you to forgive. It works very hard at that. It tries to make you feel justified in being bitter. Have you ever felt justified in being bitter about something? Just look what they did to me! I deserve to be bitter! This verse gives us very powerful insight on bitterness.

> Hebrews 12:15 *See to it that no one misses out on God's grace, that no root of bitterness springing up causes trouble and thus contaminates many,*

There's a whole lot in that verse. It describes bitterness as a root of a weed. Why? Because it can choke out your life. What happens if you don't pull out all of a weed's roots? The weed comes back bigger and stronger. We had a thistle grow in our yard once. I thought, "I'm just going to let it grow and see what happens." Well, that thing grew to be way over my head! It became a giant thistle with spiky spines all over the place. When I finally decided to get rid of it, I had to put on thick, heavy gloves so I didn't get stabbed over and over. It all came from one little root. Also, the verse says something else. It spreads! Weed roots spread. Bitterness defiles and contaminates others. It's like a root. Have you ever tried to dig a big weed root out of the ground? It's hard, right? There are lots of tendrils in the ground, reaching very far, and you've got to get them all because if you leave just one piece of root, what happens? It comes right back. So it takes strength and effort and the right tools to get the root out.

Again that saying that I saw applies here. "Living in bitterness is like drinking poison and expecting the person you are bitter against to be harmed."

So we're going to take the test again. Close your eyes. Imagine you're at this wonderful place that you love to be at. It's got beautiful music playing. Maybe it's outside, and it's a beautiful day. The sun is shining and breezes are blowing, and there's a stream nearby. The birds are chirping. That's beautiful, right? And you've got this beautiful picnic lunch laid out there. Who do you not want to see walking down the path to join you in that picnic? Take a minute.

*****

You don't have to carry the burden of bitterness around. True forgiveness will remove these harmful thoughts and God will heal the pain you've experienced. You might not forget what happened, but the pain will go away, so it won't affect your life. We need to bind the principality of bitterness, cast out the spirits that are under it and then come back and deal with bitterness. Get rid of it.

God Loves You!

God is so adamant about forgiving because He loves you very, very much. Remember what He said in John 17:23. He loves you as much as He loves Yeshua! Now this gets hard to comprehend because Yeshua is Him. They're one, right? So, in a sense, it's saying God loves you as much as He loves Himself. Well, God is Love. There are people who don't love themselves, right? But that's not God. God is Love. He is the source of Love. So he Loves Himself. He Loves Yeshua, and, this is mind-boggling, He Loves you as much as He Loves Yeshua.

Now not only does His Word say He Loves you but it tells how He demonstrated His Love.

> I John 4:9-10 *Here is how God showed his love among us: God sent his only Son into the world, so that through him we might have life. 10 Here is what love is: not that we have loved God, but that he loved us and sent his Son to be the kapparah for our sins.*

So here's the amazing thing and why the Brit Khadasha, the New Covenant is so important to be added to the Tanakh. God says He Loves His people in the Tanakh over and over again, but He showed it in Yeshua. He demonstrated His Love by coming as a man, sacrificing His life and suffering terrible pain to make atonement for your sin and bring you forgiveness, which He offers as a free gift to all who will receive it. And that is amazing because He talks about His Love. He says this is how much I Love you, and then He demonstrated His Love by coming and giving His life, suffering terribly for your sake and for my sake. Let's just give Him some praise. Thank You, Lord! Thank You. You're amazing.

But then in the next verse, He connects back to that stuff about forgiving each other.

> I John 4:11 *Beloved friends if this is how God loved us we likewise ought to love one another*

So here's where I get to this third thing about why it is so important that we forgive each other, that we be in right relationship with each other. He Loves you! You've got that now, right? If you haven't got that yet I don't know what we could do. Go back and read the previous paragraphs again and again and pray and ask God to reveal His Love to you. He Loves you, okay?

But if God Loves you, who else does He Love? He Loves your brothers and sisters and neighbors, etc. How much does He Love them? As much as He Loves you! As much as He Loves Yeshua!

Now, you might think, "Well, does He have that much Love?" Yes!! He's God! He's got an infinite amount of Love to spread around. He never runs out of Love. Okay?

Our Conflict Hurts Him

So here's the thing. It hurts Him when He sees you in conflict with another. If you're a parent, you can relate to this. I experienced this pain when our children were in conflict with each other because I love both of them. I experienced the negative feelings both of them were experiencing. Can you relate to that? When your kids are fighting, what do you do? You can't take sides because you love them both. Hopefully God shows you which one is right, if there's a right and a wrong. But maybe there isn't a right or wrong. Maybe they're just mad at each other, and they're squabbling with each other. How about having dinner with the family and the kids are squabbling with each other? How does that work? It's a bad scene, right? So this is a third reason why it's so important to God that we forgive each other and be in right relationship with each other.

He is Inviting Us To Fellowship With Him

Now, because it is so important to Him, He puts some very, very important and well-known instructions in His Word to assure that we deal with this issue periodically. And in looking at these instructions for coming to the Lord's Table, which we're going to do, we ought to keep in mind and understand that coming to the Lord's Table is an invitation to fellowship with Him.

That's what He is all about. He Loves us. He wants us to fellowship with Him! As you read through the Bible, you will see that fellowship has a lot to do with food. It has a lot to do with eating together.

We experience that too. When you invite somebody over to dinner, that's a way of coming into closer fellowship with them. When you go out for lunch together, when you meet together and you have something to eat, it's all about fellowship. Bringing people together to dine together at the same table is about fellowship. In this case, it's the Father inviting us to join Him at the dinner table because that's where He wants to have this fellowship with us.

In Depth Look At The Verses

So now we're going to look at the verses about communion again in much more detail. We are going to look at each phrase and see how it applies to our lives today personally.

1 Corinthians 11:23 *for what I received from the Lord is just what I passed on to you—that the Lord Yeshua on the night he was betrayed took bread;...*

We know it was unleavened bread because this was spoken by the Lord during the Passover Seder.

1 Corinthians 11:24 *...and after he had made the b'rakhah he broke it and said, "This is my body, which is for you. Do this as a memorial to me";*

The b'rakhah is the blessing the "Barukh Atah Adonai Elohenu, Melekh ha-olam. Ha-motzi lekhem min ha-aretz." The Matzah, the unleavened bread is a memorial. What is that? It's something that causes us to remember something, in this case, to remember Yeshua's body. The matzah is unleavened, which symbolizes being without sin. It's striped like somebody who is beaten. It's pierced and it's broken. So it helps us to remember the body of the Lord.

1 Corinthians 11:25 *likewise also the cup after the meal, saying, "This cup is the New Covenant effected by my blood do this as often as you drink it as a memorial to me."*

So the cup of wine or grape juice is a memorial that causes us to remember Yeshua's Blood shed for the forgiveness of sins. Why is that so important? Because if you want to see the origin of this, in Leviticus 17, it says it is the blood that makes atonement for the soul. So there has to be blood.

1 Corinthians 11:26 *For as often as you eat this bread and drink this cup you proclaim the death of the Lord until he comes.*

So this is saying we proclaim Yeshua's death to who? To each other, to the lost, to the principalities of darkness because it was His sacrificial death that broke ha-satan's power over us. We proclaim that ha-satan's power over us is broken because the Lord's sacrifice paid the penalty for our sins.

> 1 Corinthians 11:27 Therefore whoever eats the Lord's bread or drinks the Lord's cup in an unworthy manner will be guilty of desecrating the body and the blood of the Lord.

Now, this is very interesting because what Rabbi Sha'ul is saying is there's a way to take the Lord's Supper, what we call in Hebrew S'udat Adonai, in an unworthy way. We want to be sure that we don't do that. You agree we don't want to do that, right?

> 1 Corinthians 11:28 So let a person examine himself first, and then he may eat of the bread and drink from the cup;

So to avoid taking the S'udat Adonai in an unworthy way, you should examine yourself before you come to His Table.

> 1 Corinthians 11:29 for a person who eats and drinks without recognizing the body eats and drinks judgment upon himself.

So you should recognize the body or you will bring judgment on yourself. That's what it's saying! Now I believe that has two interpretations, and I think they're both equally correct. First, recognizing the body means recognizing the Matzah as a memorial of Yeshua's body, broken and striped for your healing. Straightforward, right? But second, recognize the Matzah as a memorial of Yeshua's Body, His people, which is broken when there is a conflict between His body's members. You see that? And I can't say which one is more valid than the other. I think they're both valid.

1 Corinthians 12:27 Now you together
constitute the body of the Messiah, and
individually you are parts of it.

So what this means is that you need to recognize that,
not only are we all brothers and sisters, we're also all part of
the same Body, Yeshua's Body. His hands, literally we are
His hands on this planet. His feet, His arms, His mind, His
heart here on earth. Do you see that? When you recognize
this togetherness in the Body, you should see the need
for reconciliation even more, because how can the Body
survive? How could you survive if one part of your body is in
conflict with another part of your body, right?

Imagine if my left foot was in conflict with my left knee.
They're just not in agreement. So I'm going to try to walk and
my left foot is going to try to take me one way, but my knee
is going to try to go a different way. What's going to happen?
Well, I'm either going to pull a muscle, or I'm going to fall
down. Right? I would end up not even able to stand.

So if you don't examine yourself as to whether you're
recognizing that you're part of Yeshua's Body and therefore
need to be in right relationship with the rest of those who
are part of His Body, you're coming to the Lord's Table in an
unworthy way. That's pretty serious! It's desecrating His Body
and Blood and bringing judgment on yourself. It gets even
more serious. He gives a more serious explanation of this in
the next verse.

1 Corinthians 11:30 this is why many among
you are weak and sick, and some have died!

I don't know how you get more serious than that! The
result of this judgment that you can bring on yourself is
sickness and even death! So I hope you agree that each of
us needs to be sure we don't open ourselves up to this kind

of judgment by not forgiving each other. Then verse 31 is very interesting.

> 1 Corinthians 11:31 *If we would examine ourselves, we would not come under judgment.*

So what does this mean to examine yourself? It means to be open to the Holy Spirit revealing whether you have any unforgiveness or any other sin in your life. It means having what the Bible calls a contrite spirit, which God says He greatly values. A contrite spirit is open to the Holy Spirit bringing correction, conviction, Godly sorrow, and repentance.

The Holy Spirit will not bring condemnation, shame, or guilt. Who does that come from? Yes, it comes from the enemy.

> 1 Corinthians 11:32 *But when we are judged by the Lord, we are being disciplined, so that we will not be condemned along with the world.*

So when you have a contrite spirit, God will judge and discipline you. He will reveal what needs to be changed in you for your own good and for His Glory.

So now to the practical side of this. How do you know who you need to forgive and be reconciled with? I'm glad you asked. What really works, and has worked for me is that test I gave you earlier. So let's take it again.

Close your eyes. Imagine you're at this wonderful place that you love to be at. It's got beautiful music playing. Maybe it's outside, and it's a beautiful day. The sun is shining and breezes are blowing, and there's a stream nearby. The birds are chirping. That's beautiful, right? There's a beautiful picnic lunch laid out. You're with close friends and everyone is laughing a lot and having a great time. Who do you not want to see walking down the path to join in that picnic? Take a minute.

Forgiving is Hard!

How can you forgive? Forgiving is hard! Well, first you can ask the Holy Spirit to make the grace that God has shown you overflow to those who have offended you. That's kind of the basis for forgiving. But, again, don't expect to have a change in your feelings toward that person. That's not necessarily going to happen. You need to exercise your freewill and decide to forgive out of obedience and an understanding, as we've learned here, of how not forgiving will harm you. It will keep God's forgiveness from you and physically give ha-satan power to harm you, bringing this judgment upon you.

I've been hurt by others. Most people have. I know this because people come in my office and talk about the struggles of their lives. You might think you know lots of people who never got hurt. But you know what? It's not true. I've done the test. In meetings, I have asked, "How many people have been hurt by other people? Raise your hand." Then I have everybody look around. What do they see? They see that there are no hands down. Every hand is up! You're not alone. You're not the only one who's been hurt. Understand that? This is life. This is what life is like. People get hurt. Yeshua said so.

> Matthew 18:7 ... *For offenses must come, but woe to that man by whom the offense comes!*

Yeshua gave us reality. We are going to get hurt.

I've had many people hurt me. My fourth grade teacher had it in for me. She put me on trial in front of the entire class, accused me, and convicted me. I had girlfriends who broke up with me. When I became a believer, my family shunned me. It was so bad that when my father died, I arranged a service for him at a Messianic Synagogue in Florida because that's where he died, and all of my aunts and uncles were living down there, but none of them would come to the funeral because I was a believer. That hurt. Then when the Lord began to move on me to step into the ministry, there were people who opposed me becoming a rabbi here, very strongly. And worse than that, there were people who encouraged me to become the rabbi, and then as soon as I did, they left the congregation. That hurt even more! Then there were people who tried to remove me from being the rabbi. So I had my share of hurts.

And I have to confess that I've hurt other people, and I've needed their forgiveness, especially my own family. My wife and daughter can testify to that. I've had to apologize plenty of times. And I'm sure there are people in the congregation who have left the congregation whose expectations I failed to live up to, and they were hurt by that. So you're not alone. All of us have been hurt.

I have found three practical ways to help me forgive, which I'm going to share with you, and I hope they will help you forgive. The first one is to remember what Yeshua said about those who were killing Him, really torturing Him and killing Him.

> Luke 23:34 *Yeshua said, "Father, forgive them;*
> *they don't understand what they are doing.*

I found that often people who have hurt me did not understand what they were doing. They were deceived, possibly by lies about me that they had believed, or they did something that hurts me, but they didn't intend to. So that's the first is to give them God's grace in that.

Second, I found that people who have hurt me often do it out of some of the baggage that they have, some of the issues in their lives that have not been resolved, some of the things that have caused them to struggle. So I can have empathy for them. "Oh I know it's because they're struggling that they did that."

Third is what this verse that we looked at before says.

Romans 12:19 *Never seek revenge, my friends;
instead, leave that to God's anger; for in the
Tanakh it is written, "ADONAI says, 'Vengeance is
my responsibility; I will repay.'"*

I've learned that I need to forgive to release the Holy Spirit to work in that other person's life.

(Some of the following about forgiveness is kind of a repeat from chapter 7, but it bears repeating so it sinks deep into our understanding.)

Then, finally, you need to forgive yourself for mistakes that you've made. Many people struggle with forgiving themselves. They can forgive other people, but they still say, "If only I hadn't done this back then, my life would be totally different. If only I had gone to a different college. If only I had not dropped out. If only I had not married that person. If only I had married that person, life would be different." Well, you need to forgive yourself because God still has a plan for your life.

This is another one that I found that people struggle with. You need to forgive God because many people see the circumstances of their life as being God's doing, and they don't like the circumstances, so they're angry at God for that. "The family that I grew up in mistreated me. God why did You put me in that family? The place where I grew up was a place where there were a lot of gangs or something. Why did You put me there? The school I went to, the teachers I had, why did You put me in that class? Why did you put me in that fourth-grade class, God? You have to forgive God too because He has a plan for you, and He will work it all out for good.

Now here's the thing that we're going to end with before we go to prayer. Once you've forgiven a person, it's very important to understand that you don't have to trust that person. But you can be around them without it tearing you up inside, without anger boiling inside you. Broken trust takes time. It takes positive experiences and interactions for trust to be restored. You don't have to make yourself vulnerable to being hurt again just because you forgive someone. That person needs to rebuild your trust.

So let's pray about a few things, then I'm going to say a few more words.

Lord, I pray You would show us if we need to forgive anyone, alive or even deceased. Give us the grace to forgive as You have forgiven us. Show us, Lord, if we have offended anyone, and give us the courage to go to them and ask their forgiveness. Lord, forgive us for having offended anyone, alive or deceased. Thank you, Lord.

Final Preparation for Sudat Adonai

So now we're going to participate in the Lord's Supper, Sudat Adonai. You are welcome to do this, if you have entered into the New Covenant, but if you have not received Yeshua as Lord and Savior, meaning you have not entered in, you should not participate. However, if you want to receive Yeshua as Lord and Savior of your life today for the first time, this is a way you can do that. And if you do it for the first time, please contact me and let me know.

Here's a sample prayer for entering the New Covenant. Lord please forgive me for anything I have ever done that has been against Your will. Please count Yeshua's sacrificial death to pay the penalty for my sin. I make You Lord of my life, as far as I am able I will obey Your instructions for me for the rest of my life. I believe You rose from the dead and are still alive. Come into my heart, live in me, guide me, open

Your Word to me and bring me into Godly fellowship. Help me to live as one of Your children.

Now, go get your goblet of wine or grape juice and Matzah, if you have some. If not, get something unleavened like a cracker, if possible. If not, bread will do. Get them ready and come back to the book with them.

So now, let's take some time again to listen to the Holy Spirit. He'll speak through your conscience. If He tells you that someone has something against you, before you eat or drink the Lord's Supper, please go to them or call them or text or message them and ask them whether you've offended them, and if so, apologize and ask their forgiveness. Now, if you can't reach them, just tell the Lord you are going to go to them as soon as you can. If that person is deceased, forgive him and just tell God you've done it.

Now again before you partake, if the Holy Spirit says you need to forgive someone, just forgive them. You don't have to go tell them that you've forgiven them if they don't know they've offended you. Okay? But if they know they've offended you, and there's a break in relationship, please go to them or contact them and tell them you've forgiven them.

Now also, as part of judging and examining ourselves, be open to the Holy Spirit's speaking to your conscience about other iniquities, other sins for which you may need to repent, especially things that deal with relationships.

So here's a list. I just want you to be just listening to the Holy Spirit and say, "Is this something I am doing or have done? These are temptations that the enemy puts before all of us.

Judging, gossip, criticizing, controlling, rejecting, jealousy, lying, lust, fear, worry, anxiety, the fear of rejection, greed, selfishness, self-accusation, self-hatred, self-rejection, hopelessness, unbelief, and doubt. The Holy Spirit may bring some others to you.

So, let's just be quiet and just listen. If one of those things comes to your mind, just repent of it because that's what this is all about, getting clean of those things. Repent of it before God. You don't need to tell anybody else. But if it's a relationship thing, then you've got to go talk to them.

Let's pray

Father, thank You for revealing anything for which we need to repent. We take responsibility for having fallen into that temptation. Forgive us. (I'm going to read this list again.) Forgive us of unforgiveness, resentment, anger, hatred, plotting revenge. Forgive us of judging, of gossiping, of criticizing, of controlling, of rejection, of envy, of lying, of lust. Forgive us for living in fear or worry or anxiety, for living in fear of rejection, for greed, for selfishness. Forgive us of self accusation, self-hatred, self-rejection, hopelessness, unbelief, doubt. If you think of anything else, just call it out right now because I haven't necessarily got everything. Any other things we need to be forgiven of? Pride! Oh that's a big one. Neglect, coveting, regrets, unkindness.

Lord, you know all the things that we can fall into, and so we take responsibility for having fallen into any of these, and we ask you to forgive us for them. Forgive us of all of them. As Your Word says. You forgive all of our sins and all of our iniquities. You remove our transgressions as far as the East is from the West. We recognize, Lord, that we can only be forgiven for one reason. It's because You came and sacrificed Your life to give us that forgiveness. That's how important it was to You. So we thank You for Your forgiveness. We just receive it right now. We receive it. We let it wash over us.

That's Your promise and You forgive us. If we were to ask you about these sins, You would not even remember them because You say You remember them no more! So we thank You, Father.

So we renounce all of these things that we have listed here, and we command every spirit that gained any kind of power over us through these things to leave us. (Let's read through them again to cast them out.) In the Name of Yeshua, every spirit that we call out must leave! Unforgiveness, resentment and anger and hatred, revenge, judging, gossip, criticizing, controlling, rejection, envy, lying, lust, fear, worry, anxiety, fear of rejection, greed, selfishness, self-accusation, self-hatred, self-rejection, hopelessness, unbelief, doubt, unkindness, neglect, pride, (and any others that come to your mind), every one of you, we command their power over us to be broken right now, in the Name of Yeshua, in the Name of Yeshua. Their power is broken and we thank You, Lord! Thank You, Father.

We ask You, Lord, that You would refill us with Your Holy Spirit, that Your Holy Spirit would just fill up all of those places and overflow, that we would be overflowing with Your Spirit. And, Lord, we know that You warned us what happens when the house is cleansed, that the enemy tries to come back and bring worse spirits. So we just ask You to help us to resist, to keep the doors closed, to keep the windows locked, to keep our house clean, Father. Give us the gift, we pray, the gift of discerning of spirits, so that when the enemy throws thoughts at us, we can discern, Oh that's that spirit! That's that spirit of coveting. That's that spirit of pride. I'm not going to listen to that. I'm going to remove that. Thank You, Lord.

And finally, Father, renew our minds. If we've gotten into any habitual thinking along these lines and habitual thinking like self rejection, or any habitual worry or fear, any habitual thinking like pride, any habitual thinking like unforgiving. In the name of Yeshua, we ask You to renew our minds and break those habits of thought. And we will continue to work on those habits, in the Name of Yeshua.

Partaking of Sudat Adonai

So, we've done the preparation. Now we're going to come to the Lord's Table

We will recite the blessing over the juice first. Would you rise, please and hold up your goblet.

Read this blessing with me:
Hebrew: *Barukh Atah Adonai Elohenu, Melekh ha-olam. Boreh p'ri hagafen. Amein*

English: Blessed are You, O Lord our God, King of the universe who creates the fruit of the vine.

So, Father, we thank You now that You've invited us to Your table so that we can have fellowship with You, table fellowship because You love us so much. And we thank You that You told us that when we take this cup it's a memorial of the Blood that you shed for our forgiveness, for our atonement. We are so thankful, Father. So we take this now and take it as the Blood of the New Covenant.

Take a drink.

Now we'll do the blessing over the bread.
Hebrew: *Barukh Atah Adonai Elohenu, Melekh ha-olam. Ha-motzi lekhem min ha-aretz. Amein*

English: Blessed are You, O Lord our God, King of the universe who brings forth bread from the earth.

Father, we thank You for these pieces of Matzah that we

have. Even as we look at them, we can see that they're striped and pierced and bruised and broken and without leaven. And we see, Lord, that they remind us so much of Your body that was broken for us, and we remember, Lord, that a couple of these things that You endured, being striped, especially, was for our healing, and so we ask You now, Father, that as we take of this that this would be like medicine. It would be healing medicine to all who are in need of healing of whatever is attacking us, whatever is making us not perfectly healthy, that this would be as medicine for us, Father.

And we also thank You, Lord, that You gave two meanings to this. You said that this is Your body broken for us to represent Your people who are broken when there's divisions among us. And so, Lord, we ask now that as we take this that we remember that it hurts You when we have divisions among us, that it hurts You because You love each of us with that incredible Love, and You hurt when we are hurt. So we ask, Lord, that you would help us to stamp out division, to close and heal wounds, to be able to work and fellowship together without conflict between us, and when conflicts do arise, to be quick to resolve them, to have that courage. As it says in Leviticus to love your neighbor as yourself, before that it says confront your neighbor when they've offended you. So help us, Lord. Give us the courage to do that.

We pray, Lord, that even as we take this that divisions between us, rifts between us would be supernaturally healed, and we would be able to walk on together with linked arms and linked hearts, going in the same direction, supporting each other, holding each other up, and inspiring one another. So we take this now, Father, as a memorial of Your body that was broken for us.

Take and eat.

Chapter 10
THE FULL POWER OF HIS RESURRECTION

Introduction

Now that we are walking in Yeshua's Resurrection Power over our sin, and we have our hearts cleansed of unforgiveness so that now there is no one that we haven't forgiven, we are ready to walk in the fullness of the Power of His Resurrection.

If you skipped ahead to this chapter, I want you right now to

STOP!!

I adjure you to go back and study in depth, and personally apply to your own life, the last three chapters. If you don't, you are missing the heart of this message. If you fail to have His Resurrection Power over your own sin, and if you have any unforgiveness in your heart, the rest of His Resurrection Power will be very limited or even non-existent in your life. Read those chapters to find out why.

Let's Pray

Yeshua's Resurrection Power available to us is beyond our human comprehension. We can only understand it fully in the Ruakh, the Spirit. So first let's ask the Ruakh to help us now.

Abba Father in Heaven, we ask You to send Your Ruakh to us now to open the eyes of our heart to reveal the infinite depth of the Truth of how amazing and awesome Yeshua's Resurrection Power can be in our lives. Yeshua promised that when we ask for the Ruakh, You will give what we have asked. In Yeshua's Name we ask, and we thank You, Abba, that You will answer. Amen.

Resurrection Power Bible Verses

Remember that the Word of Elohim is living and powerful and accomplishes the purpose for which He sends it. So let the power of the following Scriptures do their work in your heart.

These verses[9] are given in progression. Some of them we have already gone over, but they are here for us to let the Truth in them come alive and go deeper into our inner being and bring awesome power and growth in our lives and ministries.

Isaiah 25:8 (KJV) *He will swallow up death in victory;*

Romans 6:9 *We know that the Messiah has been raised from the dead, never to die again; death has no authority over Him.*

John 11:25-26 (TLV) *Yeshua said to her, "I am the resurrection and the life! Whoever believes in Me, even*

---

9   As is already done in the TLV, divine pronouns are capitalized

if he dies, shall live. 26 And whoever lives and believes in Me shall never die. Do you believe this?"

1 Corinthians 15:21-22 (TLV) *For since death came through a man, the resurrection of the dead also has come through a Man.22 For as in Adam all die, so also in Messiah will **all be made alive**.*

1 Corinthians 6:14 (TLV) *Now God raised up the Lord and **will also raise us up** by His power.*

1 Peter 1:3 (TLV) *Blessed be the God and Father of our Lord Yeshua the Messiah! In His great mercy He caused us to be born again to a **living hope** through the resurrection of Messiah Yeshua from the dead.*

Romans 1:1b-4 (TLV) *...the Good News of God, 2 which He announced beforehand through His prophets in the Holy Scriptures. 3 Concerning His Son, He came into being from the seed of David according to the flesh. 4 He was appointed Ben-Elohim (Son of God) in power according to the Ruach of holiness, by the resurrection from the dead. He is Messiah Yeshua our Lord.*

Romans 6:3-5, 11 *Don't you know that those of us who have been immersed into the Messiah Yeshua have been immersed into His death? 4 Through immersion into His death we were buried with Him; so that just as, through the glory of the Father, the Messiah was raised from the dead, likewise **we too might live a new life**. 5 For if we have been united with Him in a death like His, **we will also be united with Him in a resurrection like His**. ... 11 In the same way, consider yourselves to be dead to sin but **alive for God**, by your union with the Messiah Yeshua.*

Phil. 3:10-12 (TLV) *My aim is to know Him and the **power of His resurrection** and the sharing of His sufferings, becoming like Him in His death— 11 if somehow I might arrive at the resurrection from among the dead. 12 Not that I have already obtained this or*

*been perfected, but **I press on** if only I might take hold
of that for which Messiah Yeshua took hold of me.*

Matthew 28:18 *Yeshua came and talked with them. He
said, "**All authority in heaven and on earth has been
given to Me**.*

Luke 10:19-20 (TLV)   *Behold, **I have given you authority** to trample upon serpents and scorpions, and
over all the power of the enemy; nothing will harm
you.* [This is so awesome, but don't forget this next
verse.] *20 Nevertheless, do not rejoice that the spirits
submit to you, but rejoice that your names have been
written in the heavens.*

Colossians 3:1-4 *So if you were **raised along with
the Messiah,** then seek the things above, where the
Messiah is sitting at the right hand of God. 2 Focus
your minds on the things above, not on things here on
earth. 3 **For you have died, and your life is hidden
with the Messiah in God**. 4 When the Messiah, who
is our life, appears, then you too will appear with Him in
glory!*

His Resurrection Power in us

Let's focus now on this verse again where Sha'ul speaks
about this Resurrection Power being in us.

Ephesians 1:18-20 *I pray that He will give light to
the eyes of your hearts, so that you will understand the <u>hope</u> to which He has called you, <u>what
rich glories there are in the inheritance He has
promised His people,</u> 19 and how surpassingly
great is His power working in us who trust Him. It
works with the same mighty strength He used 20
when He worked in the Messiah to <u>raise Him from
the dead</u>....*

So it's that same power of God that raised Messiah from
the dead that works in us. We need to fully grasp this and

keep it in the forefront of our minds. We need to be reminded of it every year if not more often.

Because we are resurrected into this new Life as born again believers, God's power working in us is the same *"mighty strength"* He used to resurrect Messiah. It is the power to **over-rule all laws of nature** that God Himself established, and it is the **power to unlock the gates of hell** and death and **rescue people** held captive. But even more:

> Ephesians 1:20 *...and seat Him at His right hand in heaven,*

God's power working in us is the same *"mighty strength"* He used to not only resurrect the Messiah but to seat Him at His right hand.

> Ephesians 1:21 *far above every ruler, authority, power, dominion or any other name that can be named either in the 'olam hazeh* (these days) *or in the 'olam haba* (days to come).

God used this power to place Yeshua in the **highest possible position of authority,** and He wants to use this same power to place us there also, seated with Messiah.

> Ephesians 2:4-6 *But God is so rich in mercy and loves us with such intense love 5 that, even when we were dead because of our acts of disobedience, He brought us to life along with the Messiah - it is by grace that you have been delivered. 6 That is, God raised us up with the Messiah Yeshua and* **seated us with Him in heaven**....

We are seated with Him in heaven **"far above every ruler"** of darkness. We are seated with Him in the **position of authority over all the power of the enemy.** Imagine what our life would be like if we lived in that Living relationship power daily!

How would your life be different if you walked daily in this power? There would be no limit to what you could do for Him in what He has called you to do in His Kingdom!

Yeshua said we would do greater things than He did while He walked this earth!

> John 14:12-14 (TLV) *Amen, amen I tell you, he who puts his trust in Me,* **the works that I do he will do; and greater than these he will do***, because I am going to the Father. 13 And whatever you ask in My name, that I will do, so that the Father may be glorified in the Son. 14 If you ask Me anything in My name, I will do it."*

Wow! That is mind-blowing! Think of all the things Yeshua did! He healed. He raised the dead! He calmed storms. He fed thousands. He turned hearts to give up all and follow Him.

His apostles proved His Words true! They did mighty works in His Name and signs and wonders followed them. Even their shadows touching people brought healing. They led thousands upon thousands to repentance, to giving their lives to Yeshua. They "turned the world upside down" (Acts 17:6) for the Kingdom of Heaven.

We should be giving thanks every day that He has made this provision for us and that He designed it that we be reminded of this at least once a year on Firstfruits!

Let's pray along with Rabbi Sha'ul that we learn to walk and minister in this awesome power that God has made available to us through Yeshua's Resurrection.

> Ephesians 3:16-19 *I pray that from the treasures of His glory* **He will empower you** *with inner strength by His Spirit, 17 so that the Messiah may live in your hearts through your trusting. Also I pray that you will be rooted and founded in love, 18 so that you, with all God's people, will be given strength to grasp the breadth, length, height and*

> *depth of the Messiah's love, 19 yes, to know it,*
> *even though it is beyond all knowing, **so that you***
> ***will be filled with all the fullness of God.***

May we see these things come to pass in our ministry for
His Kingdom and His Glory that defy imagination.

> *20 Now to Him who **by His power working in us***
> ***is able to do far beyond anything we can ask***
> ***or imagine,** 21 to Him be glory in the Messianic*
> *Community [TLV: community of believers] and in*
> *the Messiah Yeshua from generation to genera-*
> *tion forever. Amen.*

> II Thessalonians 3:1 (NRSV) *Finally ...pray for us,*
> *so that the Word of the Lord may spread rapidly*
> *and be glorified everywhere...*

> Colossians 1:25 *The work is to make fully known*
> *the message* [Word] *from God*

The Whole Goal of His Resurrection Power

The whole purpose of Yeshua's Resurrection Power is
stated here so beautifully by Yeshua Himself. He appeared to
Rabbi Sha'ul in HIs Resurrected body and spoke to him.

> Acts 26:17b-18 *I am sending you 18 to open their*
> *eyes; so that they will turn from darkness to light,*
> *from the power of the Adversary to God, and thus*
> *receive forgiveness of sins and a place among*
> *those who have been separated for holiness by*
> *putting their trust in Me.*

Isn't it beautiful? Isn't it the deepest longing of our hearts
to bring people to Him—to bring them out of darkness into
His marvelous light?!

> I Peter 2:9 (NKJV)...*you are a chosen generation,*
> *a royal priesthood, a holy nation, His own special*
> *people, that you may proclaim the praises of Him*
> *who called you **out of darkness into His marvel-***
> ***ous light***

II Corinthians 4:6 *For God, who said, "Let light shine out of darkness," is the One who has shone in our hearts, to give* **the light of the knowledge of the glory of God in the face of Messiah.**

Yes, the ultimate purpose for Yeshua's Resurrection Power working in us is to help us each do our part in fulfilling of the Great Commission. We will look at that more in the next chapter.

Let's Pray

Yes, Father, we want to have the power of Yeshua's Resurrection working in our lives so we can spread Your Word and make it fully known, so we can see people brought to repentance and their hearts changed and they give their lives totally to bringing people into Your Kingdom and to fighting against the forces of the enemy.

Thank You, Father, for sending us to reach the world for You. We want to obey You and go in Your power and might. We want to see people turn from darkness and come to Your Light. Help us, Father, to learn to do this. Let us see Your signs follow to cause people to listen to Your Word and receive Your life-changing Resurrection Power. In Yeshua's Name, we pray. Amen.

Chapter 11

THE GREAT COMMISSION

It's In All Four Gospels and Acts

"Just as the Father sent me, I myself am also sending you" (John 20:21). This is one of the four statements of the Great Commission which is also given in Matthew, Mark, Luke, and Acts.

> Matthew 28:18-20 *Yeshua came and talked with them. He said, "All authority in heaven and on earth has been given to me. 19 Therefore, go and make people from all nations into talmidim, immersing them into the reality of the Father, the Son and the Ruach HaKodesh, 20 and teaching them to obey everything that I have commanded you. And remember! I will be with you always, yes, even until the end of the age."*

> Mark 16:15 (TLV) *He told them, "Go into all the world and proclaim the Good News to every creature.*

> You might have memorized it this way: *"Go into all the world and preach the Gospel to every creature"* (NKJV).

> Luke 24:45 *Then he opened their minds, so that they could understand the Tanakh, 46 telling*

them, "Here is what it says: the Messiah is to
suffer and to rise from the dead on the third day;
47 and in his name repentance leading to forgiveness of sins is to be proclaimed to people from all
nations, starting with Yerushalayim."

Notice that repentance and forgiveness of sins is part of
the Great Commission.

Acts 1:8 But you will receive power when the
Ruach HaKodesh comes upon you; you will be
my witnesses both in Yerushalayim and in all
Y'hudah and Shomron, indeed to the ends of the
earth!"

Confessing and Repenting

In John, Yeshua goes on to say this.

John 20:22 Having said this, he breathed on them
and said to them, "Receive the Ruach HaKodesh!

We'll come back to this a little later.

John 20:23 If you forgive someone's sins, their
sins are forgiven; if you hold them, they are held."

Other translations say "retained." There are two ways of
understanding what this means. But before we get into that,
let's look at what Yeshua did in another passage.

Mark 2:5 Seeing their trust, Yeshua said to the
paralyzed man, "Son, your sins are forgiven."
6 Some Torah-teachers sitting there thought to
themselves, 7 "How can this fellow say such a
thing? He is blaspheming! Who can forgive sins
except God?"

What Yeshua is doing here is demonstrating His High
Priestly role of forgiving sins. And I believe that as His
disciples, we are also to declare that He forgives sins.

> 1 John 1:9 *If we acknowledge* (confess) *our sins,*
> *then, since he is trustworthy and just, he will for-*
> *give them and purify us from all wrongdoing.*

> You might remember it this way: *If we confess*
> *our sins, He is faithful and just to forgive us our*
> *sins and to cleanse us from all unrighteousness*
> (NKJV).

When we confess our sins to God, He forgives us and purifies us! When we lead a person to confess and repent to God, we are to pray with him for God to forgive him. We are to forgive him ourselves, and we are to declare that God forgives him.

Catholics have made this into a thing of the confessional, ruling that you must confess to a priest to be forgiven. Protestants don't do that. Protestants believe you can approach God yourself for forgiveness. Forgiveness can come from our own private prayer to God or in prayers before others. Either way, we receive God's forgiveness.

Regret, Guilt, and Shame

However, my experience has been that many people confess and pray to be forgiven, but don't receive God's forgiveness. What is the evidence? Guilt and shame. So many people live in regret and guilt and shame. Are you one of them? Do your past sins haunt you sometimes? You must begin to believe that God has forgiven you and has washed that guilt and that sin away. If you don't believe God forgives you when you repent, you will continue to feel guilty and ashamed about those sins. In fact, what you are actually doing is listening to ha-satan's lies, and calling God a liar.

> Hebrews 9:14 *Then how much more the blood*
> *of the Messiah, who, through the eternal Spirit,*
> *offered himself to God as a sacrifice without blem-*

ish, will purify our conscience from works that
lead to death, so that we can serve the living God!

Should you suffer from a guilty conscience if you have received God's forgiveness? No, a guilty conscience after repentance means God's forgiveness has not been received. This can be caused by spirits of guilt and shame that need to be expelled. Many, many people are under a burden of guilt and shame over past sins. They have repented, but have not received God's forgiveness. We have to stand on 1 John 1:9. Here it is again.

> 1 John 1:9 (NKJV) *If we confess our sins, He*
> *is faithful and just to forgive us our sins and to*
> *cleanse us from all unrighteousness.*

Peter (Kefa in Hebrew) declared this truth in his first sermon.

> Acts 2:38 *Kefa answered them, "Turn from sin, re-*
> *turn to God, and each of you be immersed on the*
> *authority of Yeshua the Messiah into forgiveness*
> *of your sins, and you will receive the gift of the*
> *Ruach HaKodesh* (Holy Spirit)*!*

Kefa declared to people that in Yeshua, because of His sacrifice, we have forgiveness of all our sins. As a disciple of Yeshua, filled with the Ruakh HaKodesh, he was inspired and felt responsible to declare this to the world. And we, also as disciples of Yeshua, also have this responsibility to declare forgiveness of sin. It is at the core of the Gospel message. If we don't fulfill this responsibility, I believe this would be one of the ways in which we would be causing people's sins to be retained.

> Matthew 16:19 *I will give you the keys of the*
> *Kingdom of Heaven. Whatever you prohibit on*
> *earth will be prohibited in heaven, and whatever*
> *you permit on earth will be permitted in heaven.*

Other translations say, whatever you bind or loose. If a believer holds the sins of someone else, they are retained. We can bind others by refusing to forgive them personally or by not telling them that their sins can be forgiven through Yeshua. This is a very serious thing as we just saw in chapter 8 on forgiveness. We MUST forgive those who sin against us or offend us. We must keep on forgiving. And we must obey Yeshua's Great Commission to us. We must declare the Gospel of forgiveness at the Cross of Yeshua wherever we go.

Power and Boldness

But how do we get over our hesitation and shyness that hinder us from carrying out this Great Commission? Where do we get the power and boldness and inspiration to be sent out and do this? Yeshua mentioned something very interesting right after He gave the Great Commission in John. Let's look at verse 22 again.

> John 20:22 *Having said this, he breathed on them and said to them, "Receive the Ruach HaKodesh!"*

The Hebrew word, רוח Ruakh (also spelled Ruach) means spirit, wind, or breath. Imagine Yeshua, in His awesome resurrected body coming close enough for you to feel His breath, breathing His breath on you, saying, "Receive the Ruakh HaKodesh." Just picture that for a minute! How powerful that would be!!

Did they receive the Ruakh HaKodesh? If He did this, they would have received the Ruakh HaKodesh. Some commentators say this was just symbolic. Why? Because in Acts 1:8 He tells them to wait until Shavuot when they'll receive the Ruakh HaKodesh. But, is that really what He tells them in Acts 1?

> Acts 1:4 ..*he instructed them not to leave
> Yerushalayim but to wait for "what the Father
> promised, which you heard about from me. 5 For
> Yochanan used to immerse people in water; but
> in a few days, you will be <u>immersed </u>in the Ruach
> HaKodesh!"*

He doesn't tell them they'll receive in a few days. He tells them they'll be immersed (*filled,* or *baptized* in other translations).

> Acts 1:8 *But you will receive power when the
> Ruach HaKodesh comes upon you; you will be
> my witnesses both in Yerushalayim and in all
> Y'hudah and Shomron, indeed to the ends of the
> earth!"*

And they'll receive power when the Ruakh HaKodesh comes upon them. Power for what? To be His witnesses everywhere. This power was evidently not there yet until Shavuot (Feast of Weeks). They were getting together for prayer and for doing administrative things, but they were not being a witness to unbelievers yet.

> Acts 2:1 *The festival of Shavuot arrived, and the
> believers all gathered together in one place. 2
> Suddenly there came a sound from the sky like
> the roar of a violent wind, and it filled the whole
> house where they were sitting.*

A sign of power.

> Acts 2:3 *Then they saw what looked like tongues
> of fire, which separated and came to rest on each
> one of them. 4 <u>They were all filled with the Ruach
> HaKodesh</u> and began to talk in different languag-
> es, as the Spirit enabled them to speak.*

So, the text doesn't say they <u>received</u> the Ruakh HaKodesh on Shavuot, but that they were <u>filled</u> or <u>immersed,</u>

or <u>baptized</u>. Here's how I understand this. They had already received the Ruakh HaKodesh on Ha Bikkurim, Resurrection Day, but they were immersed in the Ruakh HaKodesh and received the power on Shavuot.

We will dig much deeper into this in the Shavuot book. But the point I want to make here is that it takes immersion (baptism) in the Ruakh HaKodesh for us to receive the power to carry out the Great Commission and declare boldly the forgiveness of sins in Yeshua.

Let's look again at Yeshua's beautiful Words about this Commission.

> Acts 26:17b-18 *I am sending you 18 to open their eyes; so that they will turn from darkness to light, from the power of the Adversary to God, and thus receive forgiveness of sins and a place among those who have been separated for holiness by putting their trust in Me.*

So let's pray for that immersion and filling of the Spirit of Elohim that will bring us that power and boldness to carry out the Great Commission right now.

Let's pray

Yes, Father, we want to obey Your Great Commission, but we need the power of Your Ruakh HaKodesh to carry it out. Father, please immerse me now again with Your Ruakh HaKodesh. Fill me with Your mighty Resurrection Power that raised Yeshua from the dead that will empower me to be bold in declaring Your Word that will open people's eyes to see the darkness they are in and to turn from it and from the bondage of ha-satan to You, to Your marvelous Light, to be set free and forgiven and to find new, true Life in You.

> I Timothy 2:4 (TLV) *He desires all men to be saved and come into the knowledge of the truth.*

Father, it is Your desire that all be saved and come to know Yeshua who is "the Way, the **Truth**, and the Life." You are the One who commanded that we take Your salvation message to all nations and to the "ends of the earth."

> John 3:16 (NKJV) *For God so loved the world that He gave His only begotten Son, that whoever believes in Him should not perish but have everlasting life.*
>
> 2 Peter 3:9 (NIV) *The Lord ... is patient with you, not wanting anyone to perish, but everyone to come to repentance.*

We thank You so much, Father, that You Love the whole world, and You don't want any to perish! We pray, Father, that You will receive Your deep desire. We pray that all people WILL come to You in repentance and receive You.

Father, fill us with Your Love for people. Fill our hearts so full of Your Love and Your compassion for unbelievers that we will long from the depth of our hearts to tell them about You. Deliver us from the spirit of timidity and shyness. Forgive us, Father, for allowing timidity to hinder us from doing Your work.

Help us to take the time to saturate ourselves with Your Word, so Your Ruakh can put the exact verses in our minds and on our tongues that will reach each person's heart. Fill us with spiritual boldness and guide us to divine encounters with people whose hearts You have made ready to receive.

> Isaiah 62:10 *Go through, go through the gates Clear the way for the people! Build up, build up the highway! Remove the stones. Lift up a banner over the peoples.*
>
> Isaiah 57:14 *"Build up, build up, prepare the way remove every stumbling block out of the way of My people."*

Matthew 24:14 *"And this Good News about the Kingdom will be announced throughout the whole world as a witness to all the Goyim. It is then that the end will come."*

Father, help us as Your servants to reach the whole world with Your Word and bring them into Your Kingdom. Your people have been doing this for 2000 years. But we need to keep on doing it, going out and spreading Your Word until the whole world knows.

Help us, Father. Guide us. Convict us. Show us what our part is, and help us to fulfill it. Help us to remove every obstruction, every hindrance that keeps people from turning to You.

Help us now, especially, in this time. At this writing, the whole world is in lock down from the virus pandemic, but Father, You have provided the internet. Help us to use online tools the best way possible to reach the most people for You. We pray for global revival in this time. This pandemic seems to be clearing everything from people's schedules that makes them too busy. Now they have time to focus on You. Protect them, Abba, from all the lies and deceit and scare tactics on social media. Clear the way for them to hear Your voice and sense Your Love. We pray all hearts will turn to You.

But we can't do any of this effectively without being filled with Your Ruakh and Your Resurrection Power. Fill us now. Immerse us mightily with Your Spirit and Power until rivers of Your Living water come gushing forth out of us!

Bring Your Word to pass that the Gospel will reach the whole world, and that knowing Your Glory will fill the earth *"as waters cover the sea"* (Habakkuk 2:14), so the end can come and You can take us all home to be with You forever! In Yeshua's Name we pray. Amein.

Chapter 12

COUNTING THE OMER

The Moad Explained

Yom HaBikkurim, besides being the day we are to give our firstfruits offering, is also the first day of the Moad of Counting of the Omer, the day God commanded us to begin counting the days leading up to the next Moad, Shavuot.

> Leviticus 23:15-16 *"Then you are to count from the morrow after the Shabbat, from the day that you brought the omer of the wave offering, seven complete Shabbatot. 16 Until the morrow after the seventh Shabbat you are to count fifty days, and then present a new grain offering to Adonai.*

So Yom HaBikkurim, Resurrection Day not only occurs in the midst of the **seven day** Moad of Matzah (Feast of Unleavened Bread), but also begins the period of **seven weeks** of counting each day. The Jewish leaders have taken this literally, just like they have taken other commandments literally, like for instance the commandment to "bind" the commandments *"on your hand, and they shall be as frontlets between your eyes,"* and thus the practice of binding phylacteries (which contain Scripture) every day. The tradition for Counting the Omer is to count each day with a special blessing.

So if you are reading this on Resurrection Day or during any of the fifty days of Counting the Omer, and you haven't done it yet, how about you stop right now and do the counting in obedience to this command of Adonai.

So take a minute to look at the list below to figure out what the traditional words are for the day you are in. The first part is for each day, given in Hebrew then English. The last sentence needs to be specific for each day. After you have it figured out, then stand up and say the blessing with me, please.

The Blessing for Counting the Omer

This first part is spoken every day:

Hebrew:
Barukh Ata ADONAI Elohenu melekh ha-olam
Asher qee'd'shanu b'mitz-votav,
V'tzee-vanu al sefirat ha-Omer.

English:
Blessed are You, Adonai our Elohim, King of the Universe who has sanctified us with Your commandments and commanded us concerning the counting of the Omer.

Specific for each day

Figure out what day you are in, then find out what to say:

Day 1
Ha-yom yom echad l' omer
Today is one day of the Omer.
Day 2
Ha-yom shnei yomim l' omer
Today is two days of the Omer.
Days 3-6
Ha-yom _____ yomim l' omer
Today is _(3-6)_ days of the Omer

Day 7
Ha-yom sheva-ah, shehem shevuah echad b'Omer.
Today is seven days, which is one week of the Omer.

Days 8-14
Ha-yom _____ *shehem shevuah echad b'Omer.*
Today is _(8-14)_ days, which is one week of the Omer.

Days 15-50
Ha-yom _____, *shehem* _____ *shevuot b'Omer.*
Today is _(15-50)_ days, which is _(2-7)_ weeks of the Omer.

Amen

The Reason

So why would God want people to be counting the days leading up to Shavuot? If someone says about an event, "I'm counting the days" it usually means they are looking forward to something really awesome. They might be counting the days until they change jobs or until their retirement. Or they might be counting the days until their graduation from high school or college. Or best of all, they might be counting the days until their wedding or till a new baby's due date! So let's see if there is something amazing we are supposed to be counting the days for in excitement and anticipation.

> Exodus 19:1 (NKJV) *in the third month after the children of Israel had gone out of the land of Egypt. On the same day they came to the wilderness of Sinai.*

Since before the time of Yeshua, Jewish scholars have interpreted that phrase "on the same day" to mean the children of Israel arrived at the wilderness of Sinai on the first day of the third month of the year, the month of Sivan. Then if you continue to read in Exodus 19, you realize that a couple of days went by, different things happened. Then the Lord told them to prepare for three days to meet Him, and then the Lord came down on Mount Sinai around the sixth day of the month of Sivan. Depending on what day of the week Passover falls, it would be on the 5th, 6th or 7th day when Shavuot occurs.

So what happened on Mount Sinai? God came down in fire and smoke and lightning and thunder and the mountain shaking and the blast of the Heavenly Shofar!!! WHOA! Think about it! It's really big! Right?!! I mean, God spoke the Ten Commandments from the mountain directly to the people! But an even bigger way of thinking about this is that's when He started to give us the Bible! It was the beginning of God giving us His Word! So that's a pretty amazing thing.

So now let's look at the New Covenant, and we will find another overwhelmingly awesome event that occurred on Shavuot. Pentecost! How do we know Pentecost happened on Shavuot? Because the Greek word, Pentecost means 50 as in counting the 50 days. It is the Greek term for the Moad, Shavuot. Shavuot means weeks (the Feast of Weeks--Shavuot), and is a form of the word seven. So it can also mean sevens, implying seven sevens. So both words are based on numbers for counting, as in the Counting of the Omer.

So two of the most important events in the history of mankind occurred on Shavuot! The giving of God's Word on Mt. Sinai and the outpouring of / immersion in the Ruakh HaKodesh / Holy Spirit, following Yeshua's sacrifice on the Cross, and His Resurrection. On Shavuot, 50 days after the Resurrection, the Ruakh came to dwell in and overflow every believer.

So I definitely would say, and I'm sure you would too, that the beginning of the giving of the Word of God and the beginning of the outpouring of the Ruakh are both remembrances very much worth counting the days until we celebrate their occurrences. Right? So on Resurrection Day

- Yom HaBikkurim - the Day of Firstfruits, we begin excitedly counting the days and looking forward to celebrating the Word and the Ruakh. I mean the Resurrection is already exciting and amazing enough to be exuberantly joyful about, but Adonai wants us to get even more excited about being filled with His Spirit because His death and Resurrection enabled that to happen. Without the Cross and the empty tomb, there would be no Pentecost! It is only by being cleansed in His atoning Blood that we can be made pure so that His presence can dwell within us. And it is by His Ruakh in us that we can begin to understand His Word!

The traditional church has two countdown periods, Advent for anticipating Yeshua's birth and Lent for preparing our hearts for commemorating the Crucifixion and Resurrection. But God only commanded one counting, and it isn't either one of those. Those two countings are nice. Those two seasons are of highest importance (even if the date of the birth is off), but God wants us to mark two other vitally important events for believers with a counting, Pentecost and Mt. Sinai!

So on Resurrection Day, let's begin the counting and ask Him what we should be studying and meditating on as we anticipate the two glorious events. We will help you do that in our next two books in this Appointed Times Series: *Counting the Omer,* and *Shavuot.*

Appendix A

Yeshua's Death and Resurrection, Scripture Chart/Timeline

Matt. 26

30 ...they went out to the **Mount of Olives** 31 Then saith Jesus unto them, All ye shall be offended because of me this night: for it is written, I will smite the shepherd, and the sheep of the flock shall be scattered abroad. 32 But after I am risen again, I will go before you into Galilee.

33 Peter answered and said unto him, Though all men shall be offended because of thee, yet will I never be offended.
34 Jesus said unto him, Verily I say unto thee, That this night, before the cock crow, thou shalt deny me thrice.
35 Peter said unto him, Though I should die with thee, yet will I not deny thee. Likewise also said all the disciples.

36 Then cometh Jesus with them unto **a place** called **Gethsemane,** and saith unto the disciples, Sit ye here, while I go and pray yonder. 37 And he took with him Peter and the two sons of Zebedee, and began to be sorrowful and very heavy. 38 Then saith he unto them, My soul is exceeding sorrowful, even unto death: tarry ye here, and watch with me. 39 And he went a little further, and fell on his face, and prayed, saying, O my Father, if it be possible, let this cup pass from me: nevertheless not as I will, but as thou wilt. 40 And he cometh unto the disciples, and findeth them asleep, and saith unto Peter, What, could ye not watch with me one hour? 41 Watch and pray, that ye enter not into temptation: the spirit indeed is willing, but the flesh is weak. 42 He went away again the second time, and prayed, saying, O my Father, if this cup may not pass away from me, except I drink it, thy will be done. 43 And he came and found them asleep again: for their eyes were heavy. 44 And he left them, and went away again, and prayed the third time, saying the same words.

45 Then cometh he to his disciples, and saith unto them, Sleep on now, and take your rest: behold, the hour is at hand, and the Son of man is betrayed into the hands of sinners. 46 Rise, let us be going: behold, he is at hand that doth betray me.

Mark 14

26 ...they went out to the **Mount of Olives**. 27 And Jesus saith unto them, All ye shall be offended because of me this night: for it is written, I will smite the shepherd, and the sheep shall be scattered. 28 But after that I am risen, I will go before you into Galilee.

29 But Peter said unto him, Although all shall be offended, yet will not I.
30 And Jesus saith unto thee, Verily I say unto thee, That this day, even in this night, before the cock crow twice, thou shalt deny me thrice. 31 But he spake the more vehemently, If I should die with thee, I will not deny thee in any wise. Likewise also said they all.

32 And they came to **a place** which was named **Gethsemane:** and he saith to his disciples, Sit ye here, while I shall pray. 33 And he taketh with him Peter and James and John, and began to be sore amazed, and to be very heavy; 34 And saith unto them, My soul is exceeding sorrowful unto death: tarry ye here, and watch. 35 And he went forward a little, and fell on the ground, and prayed that, if it were possible, the hour might pass from him. 36 And he said, Abba, Father, all things are possible unto thee; take away this cup from me: nevertheless not what I will, but what thou wilt. 37 And he cometh, and findeth them sleeping, and saith unto Peter, Simon, sleepest thou? couldest not thou watch one hour? 38 Watch ye and pray, lest ye enter into temptation. The spirit truly is ready, but the flesh is weak. 39 And again he went away, and prayed, and spake the same words. 40 And when he returned, he found them asleep again, (for their eyes were heavy,) neither wist they what to answer him.

41 And he cometh the third time, and saith unto them, Sleep on now, and take your rest: it is enough, the hour is come; behold, the Son of man is betrayed into the hands of sinners. 42 Rise up, let us go; lo, he that betrayeth me is at hand.

Luke 22	John 18
39 On leaving, Yeshua went as usual to the **Mount of Olives**; and the talmidim followed him.	1 When Jesus had spoken these words, he went forth with his disciples **over the brook Cedron (Kidron)**,
40 And when he was at **the place**, he said unto them, Pray that ye enter not into temptation. 41 And he was withdrawn from them about a stone's cast, and kneeled down, and prayed, 42 Saying, Father, if thou be willing, remove this cup from me: nevertheless not my will, but thine, be done. 43 And there appeared an angel unto him from heaven, strengthening him. 44 And being in an agony he prayed more earnestly: and his sweat was as it were great **drops of blood falling down** to the ground. 45 And when he rose up from prayer, and was come to his disciples, he found them sleeping for sorrow,	1 (cont.) where was **a garden**, into the which he entered, and his disciples. 2 And Judas also, which betrayed him, knew the place: for Jesus ofttimes resorted thither with his disciples.
46 And said unto them, Why sleep ye? rise and pray, lest ye enter into temptation.	

Matt. 26 (cont.)

47 And while he yet spake, lo, Judas, one of the twelve, came, and with him a great multitude with swords and staves, from the chief priests and elders of the people.

48 Now he that betrayed him gave them a sign, saying, Whomsoever I shall **kiss**, that same is he: hold him fast. 49 And forthwith he came to Jesus, and said, Hail, master; and **kissed him.**

50 And Jesus said unto him, Friend, wherefore art thou come? Then came they, and laid hands on Jesus, and took him.

51 And, behold, one of them which were with Jesus stretched out his hand, and drew his sword, and struck a servant of the high priest's, and **smote off his ear.** 52 Then said Jesus unto him, Put up again thy sword into his place: for all they that take the sword shall perish with the sword.

53 Thinkest thou that I cannot now pray to my Father, and he shall presently give me more than **twelve legions of angels**? 54 But how then shall the Scriptures be fulfilled, that thus it must be?

55 In that same hour said Jesus to the multitudes, **Are ye come out as against a thief with swords and staves for to take me?** I sat daily with you teaching in the Temple, and ye laid no hold on me. 56 But all this was done, that the Scriptures of the prophets might be fulfilled. Then all the disciples forsook him, and fled.

Mark 14 (cont.)

43 And immediately, while he yet spake, cometh Judas, one of the twelve, and with him a great multitude with swords and staves, from the chief priests and the scribes and the elders.

44 And he that betrayed him had given them a token, saying, Whomsoever I shall **kiss,** that same is he; take him, and lead him away safely. 45 And as soon as he was come, he goeth straightway to him, and saith, Master, master; and **kissed him**.

46 And they laid their hands on him, and took him.

47 And one of them that stood by drew a sword, and smote a servant of the high priest, and **cut off his ear.**

48 And Jesus answered and said unto them, **Are ye come out, as against a thief, with swords and with staves to take me?** 49 I was daily with you in the temple teaching, and ye took me not: but the Scriptures must be fulfilled.

50 And they all forsook him, and fled.

51 And there followed him a certain young man, having a linen cloth cast about his naked body; and the young men laid hold on him: 52 And he left the linen cloth, and fled from them naked.

Luke 22 (cont.)

47 And while he yet spake, behold a multitude,

John 18 (cont)

3 Judas then, having received a band of men and officers from the chief priests and Pharisees, cometh thither with lanterns and torches and weapons.

47 (cont.) and he that was called Judas, one of the twelve, went before them, and drew near unto Jesus to **kiss him.** 48 But Jesus said unto him, Judas, betrayest thou the Son of man with **a kiss?**

4 Jesus therefore, knowing all things that should come upon him, went forth, and said unto them, **Whom seek ye?** 5 They answered him, Jesus of Nazareth. Jesus saith unto them, I am he. And Judas also, which betrayed him, stood with them.

6 As soon then as he had said unto them, **I am he,** they went **backward, and fell to the ground.**

7 Then asked he them again, Whom seek ye? And they said, Jesus of Nazareth. 8 Jesus answered, I have told you that I am he: if therefore ye seek me, let these go their way: 9 That the saying might be fulfilled, which he spake, Of them which thou gavest me have I lost none.

49 When they which were about him saw what would follow, they said unto him, **Lord, shall we smite with the sword?** 50 And one of them smote the servant of the high priest, and cut off his **right ear.**
51 And Jesus answered and said, Suffer ye thus far. And he touched his ear, and healed him.

10 Then Simon Peter having a sword drew it, and smote the high priest's servant, and **cut off his right ear.** The servant's name was Malchus. 11 Then said Jesus unto Peter, Put up thy sword into the sheath: the cup which my Father hath given me, shall I not drink it?

52 Then Jesus said unto the chief priests, and captains of the temple, and the elders, which were come to him, **Be ye come out, as against a thief, with swords and staves?** 53 When I was daily with you in the Temple, ye stretched forth no hands against me: but this is your hour, and the power of darkness.

54a Then took they him, and led him, and brought him into the high priest's house.

Matt. 26 (cont.)

57 And they that had laid hold on Jesus led him away to Caiaphas the high priest, where the scribes and the elders were assembled.

58 But **Peter** followed him afar off unto the high priest's palace, and went in, and sat with the servants, to see the end.

59 Now the chief priests, and elders, and all the council, sought false witness against Jesus, to put him to death; 60 But found none: yea, though many false witnesses came, yet found they none. At the last came two false witnesses, 61 And said, This fellow said, I am able to destroy the temple of God, and to build it in three days. 62 And the **high priest arose, and said unto him, Answerest thou nothing?** what is it which these witness against thee? 63 But **Jesus held his peace.** And the high priest answered and said unto him, I adjure thee by the living God, that thou tell us whether thou be the Christ, the Son of God.

64 Jesus saith unto him, Thou hast said: nevertheless I say unto you, Hereafter shall ye see the Son of man sitting on the right hand of power, and coming in the clouds of heaven.

Mark 14 (cont.)

53 And they led Jesus away to the high priest: and with him were assembled all the chief priests and the elders and the scribes.

54 And **Peter** followed him afar off, even into the palace of the high priest: and he sat with the servants, and warmed himself at the fire.

55 And the chief priests and all the council sought for witness against Jesus to put him to death; and found none. 56 For many bare false witness against him, but their witness agreed not together. 57 And there arose certain, and bare false witness against him, saying, 58 We heard him say, I will destroy this temple that is made with hands, and within three days I will build another made without hands. 59 But neither so did their witness agree together. 60 And **the high priest stood up in the midst, and asked Jesus, saying, Answerest thou nothing?** what is it which these witness against thee? 61 But **he held his peace,** and answered nothing. Again the high priest asked him, and said unto him, Art thou the Christ, the Son of the Blessed?

Luke 22 (cont.)

John 18 (cont)

12 Then the band and the captain and officers of the Jews took Jesus, and bound him, 13 And led him away to Annas first; for he was father in law to Caiaphas, which was the high priest that same year. 14 Now Caiaphas was he, which gave counsel to the Jews, that it was expedient that one man should die for the people.

54b And **Peter** followed afar off. 55 And when they had kindled a fire in the midst of the hall, and were set down together, Peter sat down among them. 56 But a certain maid beheld him as he sat by the fire, and earnestly looked upon him, and said, This man was also with him. 57 And he denied him, saying, Woman, I know him not. 58 And after a little while another saw him, and said, Thou art also of them. And Peter said, Man, I am not. 59 And about the space of one hour after another confidently affirmed, saying, Of a truth this fellow also was with him: for he is a Galilaean. 60 And Peter said, Man, I know not what thou sayest. And immediately, while he yet spake, the **cock crew.** 61 And the Lord turned, and looked upon Peter. And Peter remembered the word of the Lord, how he had said unto him, Before the cock crow, thou shalt deny me thrice. 62 And Peter went out, and **wept bitterly.**

63 And the men that held Jesus **mocked him, and smote him.** 64 And when they had **blindfolded him,** they **struck him on the face,** and asked him, saying, **Prophesy, who is it that smote thee?** 65 And many other things blasphemously spake they against him.

66 And **as soon as it was day,** the elders of the people and the chief priests and the scribes came together, and **led him into their council,** saying,

15 And **Simon Peter** followed Jesus, and so did another disciple: that disciple was known unto the high priest, and went in with Jesus into the palace of the high priest. 16 But Peter stood at the door without. Then went out that other disciple, which was known unto the high priest, and spake unto her that kept the door, and brought in Peter. 17 Then saith the damsel that kept the door unto Peter, Art not thou also one of this man's disciples? He saith, I am not. 18 And the servants and officers stood there, who had made a fire of coals; for it was cold: and they warmed themselves: and Peter stood with them, and warmed himself.

19 The high priest then asked Jesus of his disciples, and of his doctrine. 20 **Jesus answered him, I spake openly to the world; I ever taught in the synagogue, and in the temple, whither the Jews always resort; and in secret have I said nothing. 21 Why askest thou me? ask them which heard me, what I have said unto them: behold, they know what I said.** 22 And when he had thus spoken, one of the officers which stood by **struck Jesus with the palm of his hand,** saying, Answerest thou the high priest so? 23 **Jesus answered him, If I have spoken evil, bear witness of the evil: but if well, why smitest thou me?**

24 Now Annas had sent him bound unto Caiaphas the high priest.

Matt. 26 (cont.)

65 Then the **high priest rent his clothes,** saying, He hath spoken blasphemy; what further need have we of witnesses? behold, now ye have heard his blasphemy. 66 What think ye? They answered and said, He is guilty of death. 67 Then did they **spit in his face,** and **buffeted him**; and others **smote him with the palms of their hands,** 68 Saying, **Prophesy** unto us, thou Christ, **Who is he that smote thee?**

69 Now **Peter** sat without in the palace: and a damsel came unto him, saying, Thou also wast with Jesus of Galilee. 70 But he denied before them all, saying, I know not what thou sayest. 71 And when he was gone out into the porch, another maid saw him, and said unto them that were there, This fellow was also with Jesus of Nazareth. 72 And again he denied with an oath, I do not know the man. 73 And after a while came unto him they that stood by, and said to Peter, Surely thou also art one of them; for* thy speech berayeth thee. 74 Then began he to curse and to swear, saying, I know not the man. And immediately the **cock crew.** 75 And Peter remembered the word of Jesus, which said unto him, Before the cock crow, thou shalt deny me thrice. And he went out, and **wept bitterly.**

Matt. 27

1 **When the morning was come,** all the chief priests and elders of the people took counsel against Jesus to put him to death: 2 And when **they had bound him, they led him away, and delivered him to Pontius Pilate** the governor.

Mark 14 (cont.)

62 **And Jesus said, I am: and ye shall see the Son of man sitting on the right hand of power, and coming in the clouds of heaven.**

63 Then the **high priest rent his clothes**, and saith, What need we any further witnesses? 64 Ye have heard the blasphemy: what think ye? And they all condemned him to be guilty of death. 65 And some began to **spit on him**, and to **cover his face, and to buffet him,** and to say unto him, **Prophesy**: and the servants did **strike him with the palms of their hands**.

66 And as **Peter** was beneath in the palace, there cometh one of the maids of the high priest: 67 And when she saw Peter warming himself, she looked upon him, and said, And thou also wast with Jesus of Nazareth. 68 But he denied, saying, I know not, neither understand I what thou sayest. And he went out into the porch; and the cock crew. 69 And a maid saw him again, and began to say to them that stood by, This is one of them. 70 And he denied it again. And a little after, they that stood by said again to Peter, Surely thou art one of them: for thou art a Galilaean, and thy speech agreeth thereto. 71 But he began to curse and to swear, saying, I know not this man of whom ye speak. 72 And the second time **the cock crew.** And Peter called to mind the word that Jesus said unto him, Before the cock crow twice, thou shalt deny me thrice. And when he thought thereon, **he wept.**

Mark 15

1 **And straightway in the morning** the chief priests held a consultation with the elders and scribes and the whole council, and bound Jesus, and **carried him away, and delivered him to Pilate.** 2 And Pilate asked him, Art thou the King of the Jews? And he answering said unto him, Thou sayest it. 3 And the chief priests accused him of many things: **but he answered nothing.** 4 And Pilate asked him again, saying, Answerest thou nothing? behold how many things they witness against thee. 5 But Jesus yet answered nothing; so that Pilate marvelled.

Luke 22 (cont.)

67 Art thou the Christ? tell us. And **he said unto them, If I tell you, ye will not believe: 68 And if I also ask you, ye will not answer me, nor let me go. 69 Hereafter* shall the Son of man sit on the right hand of the power of God**. 70 Then said they all, Art thou then the Son of God? **And he said unto them, Ye say that I am.** 71 And they said, What need we any further witness? for we ourselves have heard of his own mouth.

John 18 (cont)

25 And **Simon Peter** stood and warmed himself. They said therefore unto him, Art not thou also one of his disciples? He denied it, and said, I am not. 26 One of the servants of the high priest, being his kinsman whose ear Peter cut off, saith, Did not I see thee in the garden with him? 27 Peter then denied again: and immediately the **cock crew.**

Luke 23

1 And the whole multitude of them arose, and **led him unto Pilate**. 2 And they began to accuse him, saying, We found this fellow perverting the nation, and forbidding to give tribute to Caesar, saying that he himself is Christ a King.

3 And Pilate asked him, saying, Art thou the King of the Jews? And he answered him and said, Thou sayest it. 4 Then said Pilate to the chief priests and to the people, I find no fault in this man. 5 And they were the more fierce, saying, He stirreth up the people, teaching throughout all Jewry, beginning from Galilee to this place.

28 Then **led they Jesus from Caiaphas unto the hall of judgment: and it was early;** and they themselves went not into the judgment hall, **lest they should be defiled; but that they might eat the passover.** 29 Pilate then went out unto them, and said, What accusation bring ye against this man? 30 They answered and said unto him, If he were not a malefactor, we would not have delivered him up unto thee. 31 Then said Pilate unto them, Take ye him, and judge him according to your law. The Jews therefore said unto him, It is not lawful for us to put any man to death: 32 That the saying of Jesus might be fulfilled, which he spake, signifying what death he should die.

Matt. 27 (cont.)   Mark 15 (cont.)

3 Then **Judas**, which had betrayed him, when
he saw that he was condemned, repented
himself, and brought again the **thirty pieces of
silver** to the chief priests and elders, 4 Saying,
I have sinned in that I have betrayed the
innocent blood. And they said, What is that to
us? see thou to that. 5 And **he cast down the
pieces of silver in the temple,** and departed,
and went and hanged himself. 6 And the chief
priests took the silver pieces, and said, **It is
not lawful for to put them into the treasury,
because it is the price of blood. 7 And they
took counsel, and bought with them the potter's field, to bury strangers in.** 8 Wherefore
that field was called, The field of blood, unto
this day. 9 Then was fulfilled that which was
spoken by Jeremy the prophet, saying, And
they took the thirty pieces of silver, the price
of him that was valued, whom they of the children of Israel did value; 10 And gave them for
the potter's field, as the Lord appointed me.

11 And Jesus stood before the governor: and
the governor asked him, saying, Art thou the
King of the Jews? And Jesus said unto him,
Thou sayest. 12 And **when he was accused
of the chief priests and elders, he answered
nothing.**

Luke 23 (cont.)   John 18 (cont)

6 When Pilate heard of Galilee, he asked whether the man were a Galilaean. 7 And as soon as he knew that he belonged unto Herod's jurisdiction, **he sent him to Herod,** who himself also was at Jerusalem at that time. 8 And when Herod saw Jesus, he was exceeding glad: for he was desirous to see him of a long season, because he had heard many things of him; and he hoped to have seen some miracle done by him. 9 Then he questioned with him in many words; but he answered him nothing. 10 And the <u>chief priests and scribes stood and vehemently accused him</u>.

11 And Herod with his men of war set him at nought, and **mocked him**, and arrayed him in a **gorgeous robe**, and sent him again to Pilate. 12 And the same day Pilate and Herod were made friends together: for before they were at enmity between themselves.

13 And Pilate, when he had called together the chief priests and the rulers and the people, 14 Said unto them, Ye have brought this man unto me, as one that perverteth the people: and, behold, I, having examined him before you, have **found no fault in this man** touching those things whereof ye accuse him: 15 No, nor yet Herod: for I sent you to him; and, lo, nothing worthy of death is done unto him.

33 Then Pilate entered into the judgment hall again, and called Jesus, and said unto him, Art thou the King of the Jews? 34 **Jesus answered him, Sayest thou this thing of thyself, or did others tell it thee of me?** 35 Pilate answered, Am I a Jew? Thine own nation and the chief priests have delivered thee unto me: what hast thou done? 36 **Jesus answered, My kingdom is not of this world: if my kingdom were of this world, then would my servants fight,**

Matt. 27 (cont.)

13 Then said Pilate unto him, Hearest thou not how many things they witness against thee? 14 And he answered him to never a word; insomuch that the governor marvelled greatly.

15 Now **at that feast the governor was wont to release unto the people a prisoner,** whom they would. 16 And they had then a notable prisoner, called Barabbas. 17 Therefore when they were gathered together, Pilate said unto them, Whom will ye that I release unto you? Barabbas, or Jesus which is called Christ? 18 For he knew that for envy they had delivered him.

19 When he was set down on the judgment seat, **his wife** sent unto him, saying, Have thou nothing to do with that just man: for I have suffered many things this day **in a dream because of him.**

20 But the chief priests and elders persuaded the multitude that they should ask **Barabbas,** and destroy Jesus. 21 The governor answered and said unto them, Whether of the twain will ye that I release unto you? They said, **Barabbas.**

22 Pilate saith unto them, What shall I do then with Jesus which is called Christ? They all say unto him, **Let him be crucified.** 23 And the governor said, Why, what evil hath he done? But they cried out the more, saying, **Let him be crucified.**

24 When **Pilate** saw that he could prevail nothing, but that rather a tumult was made, he took water, and **washed his hands** before the multitude, saying, I am innocent of the blood of this just person: see ye to it.

25 Then answered all the people, and said, **His blood be on us, and on our children.**

26a Then **released he Barabbas** unto them:

Mark 15 (cont.)

6 Now **at that feast he released unto them one prisoner,** whomsoever they desired. 7 And there was one named **Barabbas**, which lay bound with them that had made insurrection with him, who had committed murder in the insurrection. 8 And the multitude crying aloud began to desire him to do as he had ever done unto them. 9 But Pilate answered them, saying, Will ye that I release unto you the King of the Jews? 10 For he knew that the chief priests had delivered him for envy. 11 But the chief priests moved the people, that he should rather release Barabbas unto them. 12 And Pilate answered and said again unto them, What will ye then that I shall do unto him whom ye call the King of the Jews?

13 And they cried out again, **Crucify him.** 14 Then Pilate said unto them, Why, what evil hath he done? And they cried out the more exceedingly, **Crucify him.**

15a And so Pilate, willing to content the people, **released Barabbas** unto them,

15b and delivered Jesus, when he had **scourged** him, to be crucified.

16 And the soldiers led him away into the hall, called Praetorium; and they call together the whole band. 17 And they **clothed him with purple**, and platted a **crown of thorns**, and put it about his head, 18 And began to salute him, Hail, King of the Jews!

Luke 23 (cont.)

John 18 (cont)

that I should not be delivered to the Jews: but now is my kingdom not from hence. 37 Pilate therefore said unto him, Art thou a king then? **Jesus answered, Thou sayest that I am a king. To this end was I born, and for this cause came I into the world, that I should bear witness unto the truth. Every one that is of the truth heareth my voice.** 38 Pilate saith unto him, What is truth? And when he had said this, he went out again unto the Jews, and saith unto them, I **find in him no fault at all.**

16 I will therefore chastise him, and **release him.** 17 (For of necessity **he must release one unto them at the feast.**)

18 And they cried out all at once, saying, Away with this man, and release unto us **Barabbas:** 19 (Who for a certain sedition made in the city, and for murder, was cast into prison.) 20 Pilate therefore, willing to release Jesus, spake again to them.

39 But ye have a **custom, that I should release unto you one at the passover:** will ye therefore that I release unto you the King of the Jews? 40 Then cried they all again, saying, Not this man, but **Barabbas.** Now Barabbas was a robber.

John 19

1 Then Pilate therefore took Jesus, and s**courged him.**

2 And the soldiers platted a **crown of thorns,** and put it on his head, and they put on him a purple robe, 3 And said, Hail, King of the Jews! and they smote him with their hands. 4 Pilate therefore went forth again, and saith unto them, Behold, I bring him forth to you, that ye may know that I find no fault in him. 5 Then came Jesus forth, wearing the **crown of thorns,** and the **purple robe.** And Pilate saith unto them, Behold the man!

21 But they cried, saying, **Crucify him, crucify him.** 22 And he said unto them the third time, Why, what evil hath he done? I have found no cause of death in him: I will therefore chastise him, and let him go. 23 And they were instant with loud voices, requiring that he might be crucified. And the voices of them and of the chief priests prevailed.

6 When the chief priests therefore and officers saw him, they cried out, saying, **Crucify him, crucify him.** Pilate saith unto them, Take ye him, and crucify him: for I find no fault in him. 7 The Jews answered him, **We have a law,** and by our law he ought to die, **because he made himself the Son of God.**

24 And Pilate gave sentence that it should be as they required. 25 And he **released unto them him that for sedition and murder** was cast into prison, whom they had desired; but he **delivered Jesus to their will.**

8 When **Pilate** therefore heard that saying, he was the more afraid; 9 And went again into the judgment hall, and saith unto Jesus, Whence art thou? **But Jesus gave him no answer.** 10 Then saith Pilate unto him, Speakest thou not unto me? knowest thou not that I have power to crucify thee, and have power to release thee? 11 Jesus answered, **Thou couldest have no power at all against me, except it were given thee from above:** therefore he that delivered me unto thee hath the greater sin.

Matt. 27 (cont.)

26b and when he had **scourged Jesus,** he delivered him to be crucified.

27 Then the soldiers of the governor took Jesus into the common hall, and gathered unto him the whole band of soldiers. 28 And they stripped him, and put on him a **scarlet robe**. 29 And when they had platted a **crown of thorns,** they put it upon his head, and a reed in his right hand: and they bowed the knee before him, and mocked him, saying, Hail, King of the Jews! 30 And they **spit upon him**, and **took the reed, and smote him on the head**. 31 And after that they had mocked him, they took the robe off from him, and put his own raiment on him, and led him away to crucify him.

32 And as they came out, they found **a man of Cyrene, Simon** by name: him they compelled to bear his cross.

33 And when they were come unto a place called **Golgotha**, that is to say, a place of a skull,

Mark 15 (cont.)

19 And they **smote him on the head with a reed**, and did **spit upon him**, and bowing their knees worshipped him. 20 And when they had mocked him, they took off the purple from him, and put his own clothes on him, and led him out to crucify him.

21 And they compel one **Simon a Cyrenian,** who passed by, coming out of the country, the father of Alexander and Rufus, to bear his cross.

22 And they bring him unto the place **Golgotha**, which is, being interpreted, The place of a skull.

Luke 23 (cont.)

John 19 (cont)

12 And from thenceforth **Pilate sought to release him:** but the Jews cried out, saying, If thou let this man go, thou art not Caesar's friend: whosoever maketh himself a king speaketh against Caesar. 13 When Pilate therefore heard that saying, he brought Jesus forth, and sat down in the judgment seat in a place that is called the Pavement, but in the Hebrew, Gabbatha.

14 And **it was the preparation of the passover, and about the sixth hour:** and he saith unto the Jews, Behold your King! 15 But they cried out, **Away with him, away with him, crucify him.** Pilate saith unto them, Shall I crucify your King? The chief priests answered, **We have no king but Caesar.**
16 Then delivered he him therefore unto them to be crucified. And they took Jesus, and led him away.

26 And as they led him away, they laid hold upon one **Simon, a Cyrenian,** coming out of the country, and on him they laid the cross, that he might bear it after Jesus.

17 And he bearing his cross went forth into a place called the place of a skull, which is called in the Hebrew **Golgotha:**

27 And there followed him a great company of people, and of women, which also bewailed and lamented him. 28 But Jesus turning unto them said, Daughters of Jerusalem, **weep not for me, but weep for yourselves,** and for your children. 29 For, behold, the days are coming, in the which they shall say, Blessed are the barren, and the wombs that never bare, and the paps which never gave suck. 30 Then shall they begin to say to the mountains, Fall on us; and to the hills, Cover us. 31 For if they do these things in a green tree, what shall be done in the dry?

32 And there were also two other, malefactors, led with him to be put to death.

33 And when they were come to the place, which is **called Calvary,** there they crucified him,

Matt. 27 (cont.)

34 They gave him **vinegar to drink mingled with gall:** and when he had tasted thereof, **he would not drink.**

35 And they crucified him, and **parted his garments, casting lots:** that it might be fulfilled which was spoken by the prophet, They parted my garments among them, and upon my vesture did they cast lots.

36 And sitting down they watched him there;

37 And set up over his head his accusation written, THIS IS JESUS THE KING OF THE JEWS.

38 Then were there **two thieves crucified with him, one on the right hand, and another on the left.**

39 And they that passed by reviled him, wagging their heads, 40 And saying, Thou that destroyest the temple, and buildest it in three days, save thyself. If thou be the Son of God, come down from the cross. 41 Likewise also the chief priests mocking him, with the scribes and elders, said, 42 He saved others; himself he cannot save. If he be the King of Israel, let him now come down from the cross, and we will believe him. 43 He trusted in God; let him deliver him now, if he will have him: for he said, I am the Son of God.

44 The thieves also, which were crucified with him, cast the same in his teeth.

Mark 15 (cont.)

23 And they gave him to drink **wine mingled with myrrh:** but he received it not.

24 And when they had crucified him, they **parted his garments, casting lots** upon them, what every man should take.

25 **And it was the third hour, and they crucified him.**

26 And the superscription of his accusation was written over, THE KING OF THE JEWS.

27 And with him they crucify **two thieves; the one on his right hand, and the other on his left.** 28 And the scripture was fulfilled, which saith, And he was numbered with the transgressors.

29 And they that passed by railed on him, wagging their heads, and saying, Ah, thou that destroyest the temple, and buildest it in three days, 30 Save thyself, and come down from the cross. 31 Likewise also the chief priests mocking said among themselves with the scribes, He saved others; himself he cannot save. 32a Let Christ the King of Israel descend now from the cross, that we may see and believe.

32b And they that were crucified with him reviled him.

Luke 23 (cont.)

33b and the malefactors, **one on the right hand, and the other on the left.**

34a Then said Jesus, **Father, forgive them; for they know not what they do.**

34b And they **parted his raiment, and cast lots.**

35 And the people stood beholding. And the rulers also with them derided him, saying, He saved others; **let him save himself,** if he be Christ, the chosen of God. 36 And the soldiers also mocked him, coming to him, and offering him vinegar, 37 And saying, If thou be the king of the Jews, **save thyself.**

38 And a superscription also was written over him in letters of Greek, and Latin, and Hebrew, THIS IS THE KING OF THE JEWS.

39 And **one of the malefactors** which were hanged railed on him, saying, If thou be Christ, **save thyself and us.** 40 But the other answering rebuked him, saying, Dost not thou fear God, seeing thou art in the same condemnation? 41 And we indeed justly; for we receive the due reward of our deeds: but this man hath done nothing amiss. 42 And he said unto Jesus, **Lord, remember me when thou comest into thy kingdom.** 43 And Jesus said unto him, Verily I say unto thee, **To day shalt thou be with me in paradise.**

John 19 (cont)

18 Where they crucified him, and **two other with him, on either side one,** and Jesus in the midst.

19 And Pilate wrote a title, and put it on the cross. And the writing was, JESUS OF NAZARETH THE KING OF THE JEWS. 20 This title then read many of the Jews: for the place where Jesus was crucified was nigh to the city: and it was written in Hebrew, and Greek, and Latin. 21 Then said the chief priests of the Jews to Pilate, Write not, The King of the Jews; but that he said, I am King of the Jews. 22 Pilate answered, What I have written I have written.

23 Then the soldiers, when they had crucified Jesus, **took his garments, and made four parts,** to every soldier a part; and also his coat: now the coat was without seam, woven from the top throughout. 24 They said therefore among themselves, Let us not rend it, but **cast lots for it,** whose it shall be: that the scripture might be fulfilled, which saith, They parted my raiment among them, and for my vesture they did cast lots. These things therefore the soldiers did.

25 Now there stood by the cross of Jesus **his mother,** and his mother's sister, Mary the wife of Cleophas, and Mary Magdalene. 26 When Jesus therefore saw his mother, and the disciple standing by, whom he loved, he saith unto his mother, Woman, **behold thy son!** 27 Then saith he to the disciple, **Behold thy mother!** And from that hour that disciple took her unto his own home.

Matt. 27 (cont.)

45 Now from the **sixth hour there was darkness over all the land unto the ninth hour.**

46 And about the ninth hour Jesus cried with a loud voice, saying, Eli, Eli, lama sabachthani? that is to say, My God, my God, why hast thou forsaken me? 47 Some of them that stood there, when they heard that, said, This man calleth for Elias.

48 And straightway one of them ran, and took a **spunge, and filled it with vinegar, and put it on a reed, and gave him to drink.** 49 The rest said, Let be, let us see whether Elias will come to save him.

50 **Jesus, when he had cried again with a loud voice, yielded up the ghost.**

51 And, behold, the **veil of the temple** was rent in twain from the top to the bottom; and the earth did quake, and the rocks rent;

52 And the graves were opened; and many bodies of the **saints** which slept arose, 53 And **came out of the graves <u>after</u> his resurrection**, and went into the holy city, and appeared unto many.

54 Now when the **centurion**, and they that were with him, watching Jesus, saw the earthquake, and those things that were done, they feared greatly, saying, Truly this was the Son of God.

55 And **many women** were there **beholding afar off**, which followed Jesus from Galilee, ministering unto him: 56 Among which was Mary Magdalene, and Mary the mother of James and Joses, and the mother of Zebedee's children.

Mark 15 (cont.)

33 And **when the sixth hour was come**, there was **darkness over the whole land** until the ninth hour.

34 And at the ninth hour Jesus cried with a loud voice, saying, Eloi, Eloi, lama sabachthani? which is, being interpreted, My God, my God, why hast thou forsaken me? 35 And some of them that stood by, when they heard it, said, Behold, he calleth Elias.

36 And one ran and filled a **spunge full of vinegar, and put it on a reed, and gave him to drink,** saying, Let alone; let us see whether Elias will come to take him down.

37 And **Jesus cried with a loud voice, and gave up the ghost.**

38 And the **veil of the temple** was rent in twain from the top to the bottom.

39 And when the **centurion**, which stood over against him, saw that he so cried out, and gave up the ghost, he said, **Truly this man was the Son of God.**

40 There were **also women looking on afar off**: among whom was Mary Magdalene, and Mary the mother of James the less and of Joses, and Salome; 41 (Who also, when he was in Galilee, followed him, and ministered unto him;) and many other women which came up with him unto Jerusalem.

Luke 23 (cont.)

John 19 (cont)

44 And it was **about the sixth hour,** and there was a **darkness over all the earth until the ninth hour**. 45a And the sun was darkened,

28 After this, Jesus knowing that all things were now accomplished, that the scripture might be fulfilled, saith, **I thirst.** 29 Now there was set a vessel full of vinegar: and they **filled a spunge with vinegar, and put it upon hyssop, and put it to his mouth.**

45b and the **veil of the temple was rent** in the midst. 46 And when Jesus had cried with a loud voice, he said, **Father, into thy hands I commend my spirit: and having said thus, he gave up the ghost.**

30 When Jesus therefore had **received the vinegar,** he said, **It is finished:** and he bowed his head, and gave up the ghost.

31 The Jews therefore, because **it was the preparation,** that the bodies should not remain upon the cross on the sabbath day, (for **that sabbath day was an high day,**) besought Pilate that their legs might be broken, and that they might be taken away.

32 Then came the soldiers, and brake the legs of the first, and of the other which was crucified with him. 33 But when they came to Jesus, and saw that he was dead already, **they brake not his legs:**

47 Now when the **centurion** saw what was done, he glorified God, saying, **Certainly this was a righteous man.** 48 And all the people that came together to that sight, beholding the things which were done, smote their breasts, and returned.

34 But one of the soldiers with a spear **pierced his side,** and forthwith came there out **blood and water.**

35 And he that saw it bare record, and his record is true: and he knoweth that he saith true, that ye might believe. 36 For these things were done, that the scripture should be fulfilled, A bone of him shall not be broken. 37 And again another scripture saith, They shall look on him whom they pierced.

49 And all his acquaintance, and the **women** that followed him from Galilee, **stood afar off,** beholding these things.

Matt. 27 (cont.)

57 When the even was come, there came a **rich man of Arimathaea, named Joseph,** who also himself was Jesus' disciple: 58 He went to Pilate, and begged the body of Jesus. Then Pilate commanded the body to be delivered. 59 And when Joseph had taken the body, he wrapped it in a clean linen cloth, 60 And laid it in his own new tomb, which he had hewn out in the rock: and he rolled a great stone to the door of the sepulchre, and departed.

61 And there was Mary Magdalene, and the other Mary, sitting over against the sepulchre.

***

He went immediately to the Temple in Heaven **[Hebrews** 9:11-12 (NKJV) But Christ (Messiah) came as High Priest of the good things to come, with the greater and more perfect Tabernacle not made with hands, that is, not of this creation. 12 Not with the blood of goats and calves, but **with His own blood He entered the Most Holy Place once for all,** having obtained eternal redemption.]

Matt. 12:40 For as Jonas was three days and three nights in the whale's belly; **so shall the Son of man be three days and three nights in the heart of the earth**.

***

Mark 15 (cont.)

42 And now when the even was come, because it was the preparation, that is, the day before the sabbath, 43 **Joseph of Arimathaea,** an honourable counsellor, which also waited for the kingdom of God, came, and went in boldly unto Pilate, and craved the body of Jesus. 44 And Pilate marvelled if he were already dead: and calling unto him the centurion, he asked him whether he had been any while dead. 45 And when he knew it of the centurion, he gave the body to Joseph. 46 And he bought fine linen, and took him down, and **wrapped him in the linen, and laid him in a sepulchre which was hewn out of a rock, and rolled a stone unto the door of the sepulchre.**

47 And Mary Magdalene and Mary the mother of Joses **beheld where he was laid**.

***

He conquered satan and his hosts **[Colossians** 2:13b-15 (TLV) God made you alive together with Him when He pardoned us all our transgressions. 14 He wiped out the handwritten record of debts with the decrees against us, which was hostile to us. He took it away by nailing it to the cross. 15 **After disarming the principalities and powers,** He made a public spectacle of them, **triumphing over them in the cross**]

Rev1:17b-18 I am the first and the last: 18 I am he that liveth, and was dead; and, behold, I am alive for evermore*, Amen; **and have the keys of hell and of death.**

***

Luke 23 (cont.)

50 And, behold, there was a man named **Joseph, a counsellor;** and he was a good man, and a just: 51 (The same had not consented to the counsel and deed of them;) he was of **Arimathaea,** a city of the Jews: who also himself waited for the kingdom of God. 52 This man went unto Pilate, and begged the body of Jesus. 53 And he took it down, and wrapped it in linen, and laid it in a sepulchre that was hewn in stone, wherein never man before was laid. 54 And **that day was the preparation, and the sabbath drew on.**

55 And the **women** also, which came with him from Galilee, **followed after, and beheld the sepulchre, and how his body was laid.**

56 And they returned, and prepared spices and ointments; and **rested the sabbath day** according to the commandment.

John 19 (cont)

38 And after this **Joseph of Arimathaea,** being a disciple of Jesus, but secretly for fear of the Jews, besought Pilate that he might take away the body of Jesus: and Pilate gave him leave. He came therefore, and took the body of Jesus.

39 And there came also **Nicodemus,** which at the first came to Jesus by night, and brought a mixture of myrrh and aloes, about an hundred pound weight. 40 Then took they the body of Jesus, and wound it in linen clothes with the spices, as the manner of the Jews is to bury.

41 Now in the place where he was crucified there was a garden; and in the garden a new sepulchre, wherein was **never man yet laid.** 42 There laid they Jesus therefore because of the Jews' preparation day; for the sepulchre was nigh at hand.

***

He preached to those who died in the flood
[**I Peter** 3:18-20 (NRSV) For Christ also suffered for sins once for all, the righteous for the unrighteous, in order to bring you to God. He was put to death in the flesh, but made alive in the spirit, 19 in which also **he went and made a proclamation to the spirits in prison,** 20 who in former times did not obey, when God waited patiently **in the days of Noah,** during the building of the ark,....]

***

***

He led people out of Abraham's bosom:
[**Ephesians** 4:8 This is why it says, "After he went up into the heights, he led captivity captive and he gave gifts to mankind." 9 Now this phrase, "he went up," what can it mean if not that **he first went down into the lower parts, that is, the earth?**]

***

***

***

Matt. 27 (cont.)

62 Now **the next day, that followed the day of the preparation,** the chief priests and Pharisees came together unto Pilate, 63 Saying, Sir, we remember that that deceiver said, while he was yet alive, After three days I will rise again. 64 **Command therefore that the sepulchre be made sure until the third day,** lest his disciples come by night, and steal him away, and say unto the people, He is risen from the dead: so the last error shall be worse than the first. 65 Pilate said unto them, Ye have a watch: go your way, make it as sure as ye can. 66 So they went, and made the sepulchre sure, sealing the stone, and setting a watch.

Mark 16

1 And **when the sabbath was past**, Mary Magdalene, and Mary the mother of James, and Salome, had **bought sweet spices,** that they might come and anoint him.

Matt. 28

1 **In the end of the sabbath, as it began to dawn toward the first day of the week**, came Mary Magdalene and the other Mary to see the sepulchre.

2 And, behold, there was a great earthquake: for the angel of the Lord descended from heaven, and came and **rolled back the stone from the door,** and sat upon it. 3 His countenance was like lightning, and his raiment white as snow: 4 And for fear of him the keepers did shake, and became as dead men.

5 And the **angel** answered and said unto the women, **Fear not ye: for I know that ye seek Jesus, which was crucified. 6 He is not here: for he is risen, as he said.** Come, see the place where the Lord lay. 7 And go quickly, and tell his disciples that he is risen from the dead; and, behold, he goeth before you into Galilee; there shall ye see him: lo, I have told you.

2 And **very early in the morning the first day of the week,** they came unto the sepulchre at the rising of the sun. 3 And they said among themselves, **Who shall roll us away the stone** from the door of the sepulchre?

4 And when they looked, **they saw that the stone was rolled away**: for it was very great.

5 And **entering into the sepulchre,** they saw a **young man sitting on the right side,** clothed in a **long white garment**; and they were affrighted. 6 And he saith unto them, **Be not affrighted: Ye seek Jesus of Nazareth, which was crucified: he is risen; he is not here:** behold the place where they laid him. 7 But go your way, tell his disciples and Peter that he goeth before you into Galilee: there shall ye see him, as he said unto you.

8 And they went out quickly, and fled from the sepulchre; for they trembled and were amazed: **neither said they any thing to any man;** for they were afraid.

8 And they departed quickly from the sepulchre with fear and great joy; and did run to bring his disciples word.

***   ***

Luke 24

1 Now **upon the first day of the week, very early in the morning**, they came unto the sepulchre, **bringing the spices** which they had prepared, and certain others with them.

2 And **they found the stone rolled away** from the sepulchre.

3 And **they entered in, and found not the body** of the Lord Jesus. 4 And it came to pass, as they were much perplexed thereabout, **behold, two men stood by them in shining garments:** 5 And as they were afraid, and bowed down their faces to the earth, they said unto them, Why seek ye the living among the dead? 6 **He is not here, but is risen:** remember how he spake unto you when he was yet in Galilee, 7 Saying, The Son of man must be delivered into the hands of sinful men, and be crucified, and the third day rise again. 8 And they remembered his words,

9 And returned from the sepulchre, and **told all these things unto the eleven**, and to all the rest. 10 It was Mary Magdalene, and Joanna, and Mary the mother of James, and other women that were with them, which told these

John 20

1 **The first day of the week cometh Mary Magdalene early, _when it was yet dark,_** unto the sepulchre,

1 (cont.) and **seeth the stone taken away from the sepulchre.**

2 Then she runneth, and cometh to Simon Peter, and to the other disciple, whom Jesus loved, and saith unto them, They have taken away the Lord out of the sepulchre, and we know not where they have laid him.

Matt. 28 (cont.)   Mark 16 (cont.)

9 Now when **Jesus was risen early the first day of the week, he appeared first to Mary Magdalene,** out of whom he had cast seven devils.

Luke 24 (cont.)

John 20 (cont.)

things unto the apostles. 11 And their words seemed to them as idle tales, and they believed them not.

12 Then arose Peter, and ran unto the sepulchre; and stooping down, he beheld the linen clothes laid by themselves, and departed, wondering in himself at that which was come to pass.

3 Peter therefore went forth, and that other disciple, and came to the sepulchre. 4 So they ran both together: and the other disciple did outrun Peter, and came first to the sepulchre. 5 And he stooping down, and looking in, saw the linen clothes lying; yet went he not in. 6 Then cometh Simon Peter following him, and went into the sepulchre, and seeth the linen clothes lie, 7 And the napkin, that was about his head, not lying with the linen clothes, but wrapped together in a place by itself. 8 Then went in also that other disciple, which came first to the sepulchre, and he saw, and believed. 9 For as yet they knew not the scripture, that he must rise again from the dead.

10 Then the disciples went away again unto their own home.

11 But **Mary** stood without at the sepulchre weeping: and as she wept, she stooped down, and looked into the sepulchre, 12 And seeth **two angels in white sitting, the one at the head, and the other at the feet, where the body of Jesus had lain.** 13 And **they say unto her, Woman, why weepest thou?** She saith unto them, Because they have taken away my Lord, and I know not where they have laid him. 14 And when she had thus said, she turned herself back, and saw Jesus standing, and knew not that it was Jesus. 15 **Jesus saith unto her, Woman, why weepest thou? whom seekest thou?** She, supposing him to be the gardener, saith unto him, Sir, if thou have borne him hence, tell me where thou hast laid him, and I will take him away. 16 **Jesus saith unto her, Mary.** She turned herself, and saith unto him, Rabboni; which is to say, Master. 17 Jesus saith unto her, **Touch me not; for I am not yet ascended to my Father: but go to my brethren, and say unto them, I ascend unto my Father, and your Father; and to my God, and your God.**

Matt. 28 (cont.)

Mark 16 (cont.)

10 And she [Mary] went and **told them that had been with him, as they mourned and wept.**

11 And they, **when they had heard that he was alive, and had been seen of her, believed not.**

***

9 And as **they** went to **tell his disciples,** behold, **Jesus met them, saying, All hail.** And they came and **held him by the feet, and worshipped him.** 10 Then said **Jesus unto them, Be not afraid: go tell my brethren that they go into Galilee, and there shall they see me.**

11 Now when they were going, behold, some of the watch came into the city, and shewed unto the chief priests all the things that were done. 12 And when they were assembled with the elders, and had taken counsel, they gave large money unto the soldiers, 13 Saying, Say ye, His disciples came by night, and stole him away while we slept. 14 And if this come to the governor's ears, we will persuade him, and secure you. 15 So they took the money, and did as they were taught: and this saying is commonly reported among the Jews until this day.

12 After that **he appeared in another form unto two of them, as they walked, and went into the country.** 13 And they went and told it unto the residue [rest]: neither believed they them.

Luke 24 (cont.)

John 20 (cont.)

18 **Mary Magdalene came and told the disciples that she had seen the Lord**, and that he had spoken these things unto her.

13 And, behold, two of them went that same day to a village called **Emmaus**, which was from Jerusalem about threescore furlongs. 14 And they talked together of all these things which had happened. 15 And it came to pass, that, while they communed together and reasoned, **Jesus himself drew near,** and went with them. 16 But their eyes were holden that they should not know him. 17 And he said unto them, What manner of communications are these that ye have one to another, as ye walk, and are sad? 18 And the one of them, whose name was Cleopas, answering said unto him, Art thou only a stranger in Jerusalem, and hast not known the things which are come to pass there* in these days? 19 And he said unto them, What things? And they said unto him, Concerning Jesus of Nazareth, which was a prophet mighty in deed and word before God and all the people: 20 And how the chief priests and our rulers delivered him to be condemned to death, and have crucified him. 21 But we trusted that it had been he which should have redeemed Israel: and **beside all this, to day is the third day since these things were done.**

Matt. 28 (cont.)   ***

***

*[[[**I Cor. 15:4** ...he was buried, and that
he rose again the third day according to the
Scriptures, 5 and that **he was seen of Cephas,
then to the Twelve.**]]]*

***

Mark 16 (cont.)
14 Afterward **he appeared unto the eleven as
they sat at meat,** and upbraided them with
their unbelief and hardness of heart, because
they believed not them which had seen him
after he was risen.

Luke 24 (cont.)

John 20 (cont.)

22 Yea, and certain women also of our company made us astonished, **which were early at the sepulchre; 23 And when they found not his body**, they came, **saying, that they had also seen a vision of angels, which said that he was alive.**

24 And **certain of them which were with us went to the sepulchre, and found it even so as the women had said: but him they saw not.**

25 Then **he said unto them, O fools, and slow of heart to believe all that the prophets have spoken: 26 Ought not Christ to have suffered these things, and to enter into his glory?** 27 And beginning at Moses and all the prophets, he expounded unto them in all the scriptures the things concerning himself.

28 And they drew nigh unto the village, whither they went: and he made as though he would have gone further. 29 But they constrained him, saying, Abide with us: for it is toward evening, and the day is far spent. And he went in to tarry with them.
30 And it came to pass, as he sat at meat with them, he took bread, and blessed it, and brake, and gave to them. 31 And **their eyes were opened, and they knew him; and he vanished out of their sight.**

32 And they said one to another, Did not our heart burn within us, while he talked with us by the way, and while he opened to us the scriptures?

33 And they rose up the same hour, and returned to **Jerusalem**, and **found the eleven gathered together, and them that were with them, 34 Saying, The Lord is risen indeed, and hath appeared to Simon.**

35 And they told what things were done in the way, and how he was known of them in breaking of bread.

36 And as they thus spake, **Jesus himself stood in the midst of them,** and saith unto them, Peace be unto you. 37 But they were terrified and affrighted, and supposed that they had seen a spirit.

19 **Then the same day at evening, being the first day of the week,** when the **doors were shut** where the disciples were assembled for fear of the Jews, **came Jesus and stood in the midst,** and saith unto them, Peace be unto you.

Matt. 28 (cont.)   Mark 16 (cont.)

Luke 24 (cont.)

38 **And he said unto them, Why are ye troubled? and why do thoughts arise in your hearts? 39 Behold my hands and my feet, that it is I myself: handle me, and see; for a spirit hath not flesh and bones, as ye see me have.** 40 And when he had thus spoken, he shewed them his hands and his feet. 41 And while they yet believed not for joy, and wondered, he said unto them, **Have ye here any meat?** 42 And they gave him a piece of a broiled fish, and of an honeycomb. 43 And he took it, and did eat before them. 44 And **he said unto them, These are the words which I spake unto you, while I was yet with you, that all things must be fulfilled, which were written in the law of Moses, and in the prophets, and in the psalms, concerning me.** 45 Then **opened he their understanding,** that they might **understand the scriptures,** 46 And **said unto them, Thus it is written, and thus it behoved Christ to suffer, and to rise from the dead the third day: 47 And that repentance and remission of sins should be preached in his name among all nations, beginning at Jerusalem. 48 And ye are witnesses of these things.**

49 **And, behold, I send the promise of my Father upon you: but tarry ye in the city of Jerusalem, until ye be endued with power from on high.**

John 20 (cont.)

20 And when he had so said, he shewed unto them his hands and his side. Then were the disciples glad, when they saw the Lord. 21 Then said Jesus to them again, Peace be unto you: as my Father hath sent me, even so send I you. 22 And when he had said this, he breathed on them, and saith unto them, Receive ye the Holy Ghost: 23 Whose soever sins ye remit, they are remitted unto them; and whose soever sins ye retain, they are retained.

24 But **Thomas,** one of the twelve, called Didymus, was not with them when Jesus came. 25 The other disciples therefore said unto him, We have seen the Lord. But he said unto them, Except I shall see in his hands the print of the nails, and put my finger into the print of the nails, and thrust my hand into his side, I will not believe.

26 And **after eight days again his disciples were within,** and Thomas with them: then **came Jesus, the doors being shut, and stood in the midst,** and said, Peace be unto you. 27 Then **saith he to Thomas, Reach hither thy finger, and behold my hands; and reach hither thy hand, and thrust it into my side: and be not faithless, but believing.** 28 And Thomas answered and said unto him, My Lord and my God. 29 **Jesus saith unto him, Thomas, because thou hast seen me, thou hast believed: blessed are they that have not seen, and yet have believed.**

30 And many other signs truly did Jesus in the presence of his disciples, which are not written in this book: 31 But these are written, that ye might believe that Jesus is the Christ, the Son of God; and that believing ye might have life through his name.

Matt. 28 (cont.)

Mark 16 (cont.)

16 Then the eleven disciples went away into Galilee, into a mountain where Jesus had appointed them. 17 And **when they saw him, they worshipped him**: but some doubted.

18 And **Jesus** came and **spake unto them, saying, All power is given unto me in heaven and in earth. 19 Go ye therefore, and teach all nations, baptizing them in the name of the Father, and of the Son, and of the Holy Ghost: 20 Teaching them to observe all things whatsoever I have commanded you: and, lo, I am with you alway, even unto the end of the world. Amen.**

Matt. 28 (ended)

15 And he said unto them, **Go ye into all the world, and preach the gospel to every creature.** 16 He that believeth and is baptized shall be saved; but he that believeth not shall be damned. 17 And these signs shall follow them that believe; In my name shall they cast out devils; they shall speak with new tongues; 18 They shall take up serpents; and if they drink any deadly thing, it shall not hurt them; they shall lay hands on the sick, and they shall recover.

Acts 1

1 The former treatise have I made, O Theophilus, of all that Jesus began both to do and teach, 2 Until the day in which he was taken up, after that he through the Holy Ghost had given commandments unto the **apostles** whom he had chosen:

3 To whom also **he shewed himself alive after his passion by many infallible proofs, being seen of them forty days,** and speaking of the things pertaining to the kingdom of God:

4 And, **being assembled together with them,** commanded them that they should not depart from Jerusalem, but wait for the promise of the Father, which, saith he, ye have heard of me. 5 For John truly baptized with water; but **ye shall be baptized with the Holy Ghost not many days hence.**

6 **When they therefore were come together,** they asked of him, saying, Lord, wilt thou at this time restore again the kingdom to Israel?

[[[*I Cor. 15:6* After that, **he was seen of above five hundred brethren at once**; of whom the greater part remain unto this present, but some are fallen asleep. 7 After that, he was seen of James;]]]

Mark 16 (cont.)

Luke 24 (cont.)

John 21

1 After these things Jesus shewed himself again to the disciples at the sea of Tiberias; and on this wise shewed he himself. 2 There were together Simon Peter, and Thomas called Didymus, and Nathanael of Cana in Galilee, and the sons of Zebedee, and two other of his disciples. 3 **Simon Peter saith unto them, I go a fishing**. They say unto him, **We also go with thee.** They went forth, and entered into a ship immediately; and that night they caught nothing. 4 But when the morning was now come, Jesus stood on the shore: but the disciples knew not that it was Jesus. 5 Then Jesus saith unto them, Children, have ye any meat? They answered him, No. 6 And he said unto them, **Cast the net on the right side of the ship, and ye shall find.** They cast therefore, and now they were not able to draw it for the multitude of fishes. 7 Therefore that disciple whom Jesus loved saith unto Peter, It is the Lord. Now when Simon Peter heard that it was the Lord, he girt his fisher's coat unto him, (for he was naked,) and did cast himself into the sea. 8 And the other disciples came in a little ship; (for they were not far from land, but as it were two hundred cubits,) dragging the net with fishes. 9 As soon then as they were come to land, they saw a fire of coals there, and fish laid thereon, and bread. 10 Jesus saith unto them, Bring of the fish which ye have now caught. 11 Simon Peter went up, and **drew the net to land full of great fishes, an hundred and fifty and three:** and for all there were so many, yet was not the net broken. 12 Jesus saith unto them, **Come and dine**. And none of the disciples durst ask him, Who art thou? knowing that it was the Lord. 13 Jesus then cometh, and taketh bread, and giveth them, and fish likewise. 14 **This is now the third time that Jesus shewed himself to his disciples, after that he was risen from the dead.**

15 So when they had dined, Jesus saith to **Simon Peter, Simon, son of Jonas, lovest thou me more than these?** He saith unto him, Yea, Lord; thou knowest that I love thee. He saith unto him, **Feed my lambs.** 16 He saith ... **lovest thou me?**

Acts 1 (cont.)

7 And he said unto them, It is not for you to know the times or the seasons, which the Father hath put in his own power. 8 But ye shall receive power, after that the Holy Ghost is come upon you: and ye shall be witnesses unto me both in Jerusalem, and in all Judaea, and in Samaria, and unto the uttermost part of the earth.

9 And when he had spoken these things, while they beheld, **he was taken up; and a cloud received him out of their sight.** 10 And while they looked stedfastly toward heaven as he went up, behold, two men stood by them in white apparel; 11 Which also said, Ye men of Galilee, why stand ye gazing up into heaven? this same Jesus, which is taken up from you into heaven, shall so come in like manner as ye have seen him go into heaven.

12 Then returned they unto Jerusalem from the mount called Olivet, which is from Jerusalem a sabbath day's journey.
13 And when they were come in, they went up into an upper room, where abode both Peter, and James, and John, and Andrew, Philip, and Thomas, Bartholomew, and Matthew, James the son of Alphaeus, and Simon Zelotes, and Judas the brother of James.

19 So then after the Lord had spoken unto them, **he was received up into heaven,** and sat on the right hand of God.

20 And they went forth, and preached every where, the Lord working with them, and confirming the word with signs following. Amen.

Luke 24 (cont.)

John 21 (cont.)

He saith unto him, Yea, Lord; thou knowest that I love thee. He saith unto him, **Feed my sheep.** 17 He saith ..., **lovest thou me?** Peter was grieved because he said unto him the **third time**, Lovest thou me? And he said..., Lord, thou knowest all things; thou knowest that I love thee. Jesus saith..., **Feed my sheep.** 18 Verily, verily, I say unto thee, When ... thou shalt be old, thou shalt stretch forth thy hands, and another shall gird thee, and carry thee whither thou wouldest not. 19 This spake he, signifying by what death he should glorify God. And ... he saith..., **Follow me.** 20 Then Peter, turning about, ... saith to Jesus, Lord, and what shall this man do? 22 Jesus saith unto him, If I will that he tarry till I come, what is that to thee? **follow thou me.**

23 ... 24 This is the disciple which testifieth of these things, and wrote these things.... 25 And there are also many other things which Jesus did, the which, if they should be written every one, I suppose that even the world itself could not contain the books that should be written. Amen.

50 And he led them out as far as to Bethany, and he lifted up his hands, and blessed them. 51 And it came to pass, while he blessed them, he was parted from them, and **carried up into heaven**. 52 And they worshipped him, and returned to Jerusalem with great joy: 53 And were continually in the temple, praising and blessing God. Amen.

APPENDIX B: Death and Resurrection Timeline

Here's a summary list of the sequence of events from the preceding Scripture chart:

1. Wednesday evening: Pesakh Seder,

2. Wednesday night: Garden vigil, then betrayed, arrested, accused falsely by those who were envious of His anointing

3. Thursday morning: tried, beaten, whipped, forced to carry His own cross

4. Thursday afternoon: Yeshua was crucified and died at 3 pm. His blood was poured out on the Cross, which was the final sacrifice. (See my book, *Pesakh,* and chapters 3 and 4 in this book for an explanation of why Thursday and not Friday, as the church has taught.)

5. At the moment of His death, His soul and spirit went to be with God in Heaven where He entered the Holy of Holies.

6. At that same moment, the parokhet/curtain was torn, signifying the way was opened into the Holy of Holies.

7. At that same moment, an earthquake opened the tombs of the righteous.

8. Sometime Friday - Saturday: Then He came back to earth and descended into hell, defeated hell and death, and took the keys.

9. Sometime Friday - Saturday: Using the keys, He opened the doors of Avraham's bosom.

10. Sunday morning early: His body was resurrected. Why? Because the prophesy said He had to be in the tomb how long? For 3 days and 3 nights. So it couldn't have happened until after that third night.

11. Sunday later in the morning: Miryam encountered Yeshua and physically touched His resurrected Body, but He told her not to hold onto Him because He had not yet gone to His Father (in His resurrected body).

12. Sunday: Yeshua ascended to Heaven bodily for the first time.

13. Sunday, later in the day: Many holy people bodily resurrected after Yeshua's bodily Resurrection, and they went into Jerusalem and were seen by many.

14. Late Sunday?: As He ascended (or it could've been later), Yeshua brought the people from Avraham's bosom with Him into Heaven, including those who had resurrected and appeared in the city, and those from the flood who heard His Gospel message and accepted His atonement (1 Peter 3:18-20).

www.ingramcontent.com/pod-product-compliance
Lightning Source LLC
Chambersburg PA
CBHW060046100426
42742CB00014B/2722